D1324949

INDIA

LIVING WISDOM

INDIA

RICHARD WATERSTONE

SERIES CONSULTANT: **PIERS VITEBSKY**

MACMILLAN

IN ASSOCIATION WITH
DUNCAN BAIRD PUBLISHERS

India

First published in Great
Britain in 1995

A DBP book
published by
Macmillan Reference Books
a division of Macmillan
Publishers Limited
Cavaye Place
London SW10 9PG
and Basingstoke

A CIP catalogue record for
this book is available from the
British Library

ISBN 0-333-63848-4

Conceived, created and
designed by
Duncan Baird Publishers
Sixth Floor
Castle House
75–76 Wells Street
London W1P 3RE

10 9 8 7 6 5 4 3 2 1

VOLUME CONSULTANT: PAUL
DUNDAS

Editors: Slaney Begley,
George Michell, Nigel
Rodgers, Simon Willis
Assistant editor: Lucy Rix
Designer: Sue Bush
Picture research: Nadine
Bazar

Typeset in Times NR MT
Colour reproduction by
Colourscan, Singapore
Printed in Singapore

Contents

Introduction

India is the home of one of the world's oldest civilizations. Sanskrit, its literary language, is probably the most ancient language still in use and the *Vedas,* which date back to the 12th century BC, are believed to be the oldest scriptures still in use. Modern India is a secular state in which religion continues to play an important role in daily life. This book traces the course of Indian religious traditions and practices from early Vedic belief systems through the development of Buddhism and Jainism to the pluralism of Hindu deities and worship. Other religions are also important. There are some Christians, as well as numerous ancient tribal religions. Islam established itself in northern India from the 12th century AD and reached its apogee under the Mughal dynasty (1526–1707), where it grew into a distinctive Indian Muslim culture. But the main focus of this book is on the traditions which, broadly speaking, make up what is called Hinduism. Buddhism and Jainism appear as developments from within this Hindu world.

During the 2nd millennium BC, the invading Aryans brought to India from central Asia beliefs shared with other Indo-European peoples. Central to their Vedic religion were sacrifice and a belief that the universe had to be continually recreated. From this Vedic period dates the enduring division of Indian society into four main categories: *brahmin* (priest), *kshatriya* (warrior), *vaishya* (trader) and *shudra* (labourer).

By the 6th century BC, dissatisfaction with Vedic ritual saw the emergence of sects led by philosophers who renounced the illusions of the world in favour of reaching an inner reality and *moksha* (release from the cycles of rebirth). The greatest of these philosophers were the future Buddha, Siddhartha Gautama, whose powers of concentration and insight led him to enlightenment, and Mahavira, the founder of Jainism.

Buddhism flourished during the Maurya dynasty (3rd century BC to *c*.150BC), but as the Maurya empire collapsed, so religion fragmented. The Gupta period (*c*.AD320–540) has been called the Classical Age of India, when the present styles of Indian art, literature and philosophy were established. By the 8th century AD, Hinduism had replaced Buddhism in much of southern India. Colonies of Christians and Jews were then well-established in western India, while Indian merchants had carried Indian culture and religion – both Hindu and Buddhist – across South-East Asia. Today, Hindu societies and influences are found especially in Sri Lanka and parts of Malaysia; the island of Bali in Indonesia is also Hindu.

Flaking posters suggest the profusion of imagery, sacred and secular, which forms a background to the lives of most Indians even today.

Indian Buddhists, Jains and Hindus regard the land of India itself as sacred. In a country where there are said to be 330 million gods and goddesses, divinity may also be attained by human beings. The profusion of gods and beliefs in fact reveals Indian eclecticism and tolerance. Perhaps because they are not monotheistic, but acknowledge many gods, Indian religions do not condemn outsiders as enemies of the faith; rather they try to embrace every human effort to know and worship the divine. Underlying Indian philosophy is the belief that this world is filled with sorrow and illusion, behind which lies the nameless reality of transcendent godhead. Linked with the common recognition of the authority of the *Vedas*, this belief does much to unite the many sects throughout the Hindu world.

Early India

As early as 2500BC, the Indus Valley was the centre of a flourishing indigenous culture with social and political sophistication and a pantheon of gods. Artefacts from Indus Valley sites have been found as far south as Bombay, but it was in the great cities of Harappa and Mohenjo-daro, in what is now Pakistan, that the power and influence of this civilization were best demonstrated.

When the Aryans invaded the subcontinent about 1,000 years later, they found little resistance from what was by then a decaying culture. The Aryans overcame northern India not only by military superiority, but also by their cultural and religious vigour, derived from their original homeland in central Asia. Sacrifice lay at the heart of their ritual and was based on a series of sacred texts called the *Vedas*: one of the Aryans' principal deities was Agni, Lord of the Sacrificial Fire and the Hearth. The chief Aryan gods, such as Varuna and Indra, were warrior deities whose splendour transformed what they saw as the chaotic darkness of the pre-Aryan demon realms, illuminating them with the light of Vedic righteousness and truth.

Chariots (represented symbolically by this 15th-century AD chariot-temple in Hampi, Karnataka) carried invading Aryan warriors to astonishing military victories in the 2nd millennium BC. Their reign over northern India, however, was marked by cultural as well as military prowess; their greatest legacy is the Vedas, *a prodigious body of verse, philosophy and hymns that is among the world's oldest written sacred scriptures.*

Indus Valley culture

Around the middle of the 3rd millennium BC the first civilization in India emerged with the cities of Harappa and Mohenjo-daro. The two sites, separated by 400 miles (640km), lie along the Indus river, which flows through what are now the arid plains of Pakistan, but which was then a well-watered region. The urban civilization which flourished in this area is called the Indus Valley culture. It is roughly contemporary with the cultures of Mesopotamia and Egypt, but, despite many archaeological discoveries, no written records of life in the region exist.

Most scholars now agree that, on the evidence of the regular layouts of the streets and the standard plans of houses, wells and drains, the cities of Harappa and Mohenjo-daro were both

Enigmatic motifs decorate a ceramic lid found at one of the sites in the Indus Valley.

built by a similar culture. Indus Valley artefacts have been unearthed at seventy different sites in Pakistan as well as in Gujarat and Rajasthan. The area enclosed by all the sites so far discovered is larger than modern Pakistan, pointing to a considerable empire or confederation. There is evidence of trading links with Mesopotamia.

Sir Mortimer Wheeler, the British archaeologist who excavated the sites in the early 1950s, believed them to be part of the largest "political experiment before the advent of the Roman empire", a High-Bronze-Age urban culture with a hierarchical political and social system. Certainly their achievements in sanitation rival anything the Romans later built; the Great Bath at Mohenjo-daro is 897 feet^2 (83m^2) in area; a dock for ships at Lothal is equally impressive.

Animals, especially cows, bulls and snakes, were apparently revered. It is probable that early inhabitants of the Indus Valley worshipped a goddess as well as a male fertility god, with animal sacrifice playing a major part in rituals. Many archaeologists have detected indigenous influences in the various artefacts unearthed in the region, especially what appear to be *lingas* and seals showing gods seated in a yogic position.

The decline of the Indus Valley civilization is mysterious. By the time the Aryans (see pp.12–13) entered northern India some time after 1500BC, Harappa and Mohenjo-daro had been abandoned and had fallen into ruin.

This bust of a bearded figure wearing a cloak, who is believed to be a priest, is one of the artefacts excavated at Mohenjo-daro, the largest city of the Indus Valley civilization.

PREHISTORIC YOGIC PRACTICES

Perhaps the best-known aspect of Indian philosophy and religion is the practice of yoga (see pp.82–91). It is possible that many of yoga's disciplines emerged from shamanistic practices, such as breath control and the use of rhythm, sound, drugs and dance to achieve an "inner heat" that leads to ecstasy. The yogi, seated cross-legged in the lotus posture, deep in meditative concentration, is today one of the most familiar of all images of Hinduism.

Intriguingly, seals that have been discovered at Indus Valley sites seem to indicate that some form of early yogic arts were practised in these cities more than 4,000 years ago (see below). As no written records survive, this cannot be proven. Many characteristics of shamanism, such as identification with particular animal soul-guides, the acquisition of supernatural powers, the ability to appear and disappear at will, summon spirits or survive extreme heat or cold, still serve as the basis of modern yoga in present-day India.

Six seals have been excavated from the Indus Valley sites that appear to depict figures seated in a yoga posture. Most of the seals include script which has yet to be satisfactorily deciphered. The example above shows a three-faced, seated deity, surrounded by four animals: *a tiger, a rhinoceros, an elephant and a water buffalo; a gazelle is shown in the foreground. The deity is wearing a headdress bearing three horns and his phallus is exposed. Many scholars have linked this figure with the later Hindu deity Shiva.*

The Aryans

The arrival of Aryan warriors in the middle of the second millennium BC marked a new phase in the culture and beliefs of India. As their chariots moved east, they encountered only scattered communities of hunters and farmers, for the once great cities of the Indus Valley civilization had fallen into ruin (see pp.10–11). The Aryans were vastly superior in military strength to their opponents and were filled with a confidence derived from a pantheon of glorious gods. It was this energy that inspired the poets or "seers" who wrote the *Vedas* (see pp.16–17), the collected verse and liturgy composed over the 1,000 years of Aryan hegemony. The language of these sacred texts was Sanskrit, one of the earliest known Indo-European languages.

It is uncertain as to where the Aryans began their journey, and little is known about their first thousand years in India. We can only speculate upon their

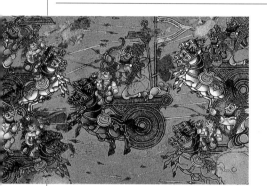

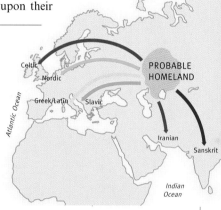

THE CHARIOT

It was the two-horse chariot that bore the Aryans victoriously in battle as they moved eastward, cutting a swathe through the less well-armed peoples whom they encountered on their way. Although the wheel had first been used in Sumer, in *c.*3200BC, the earliest chariots and carts were crude and clumsy, with solid wooden wheels that turned together, connected by a fixed axle. In war they were of limited use. By *c.*2000BC, however, lighter

Depiction of a war chariot in a 17th-century manuscript.

spoked wheels were introduced and chariots were designed with freely revolving axles. When a pair of fast horses was yoked to the chariot's front, the vehicle became an invincible weapon, and a new form of warfare was born. In the words of the mythologist Joseph Campbell, the chariot divided the world of the Bronze Age "between those who cry 'Victory' and those who weep".

THE SPREAD OF INDO-EUROPEAN LANGUAGES

Many of the languages spoken in northern India and Europe today were brought by different waves of Aryan peoples from the middle of the 2nd millennium onward (see above). Theories about an original Aryan homeland are based solely on linguistic evidence. In southern and central India, languages derive from Dravidian and Austro-Asiatic roots respectively, quite unrelated to the Aryans.

reasons for leaving their homeland: perhaps their migration from the grasslands lying between the Caspian Sea and the Aral Sea was initiated by overpopulation or their sudden displacement by other pastoral tribes, anxious to seize adequate grazing for their livestock. The Aryans were nomads, and their ancestors had probably hunted the Eurasian plains for many thousands of years. They did not possess iron nor did they build in stone, and archaeologists have little more than pottery fragments and the barest indications of occupation with which to assemble a picture of early Aryan life in India.

The era of the Aryan occupation of India coincides with the composition of the *Vedas* and is commonly known as the Vedic period. Although these sacred texts do not give clear descriptions of Aryan communities, their pantheon of chariot-riding gods, with the sun shining behind their backs as they defeat the powers of darkness, is clearly derived from a warlike, originally nomadic, culture. Their principal deities were associated with the sun rather than with the moon, and their mythologies, far from being fatalistic, engendered promises of freedom and of human victory.

Auspicious and evil swastikas in the art of Himalayan Buddhism (left) and in Nazi propaganda.

ARYAN CULTURE AND THE NAZIS

The word Aryan and the solar symbol of the swastika have never roused more fear than in 20th-century Europe. A renewed interest in paganism in late 19th-century Germany was followed in the 1930s by the Nazis' political programme of nationalism and racism, when Adolf Hitler strove to realize the supposed supremacy of the Aryan "master race". Nordic culture shares the same Indo-European roots as Vedic culture in India. Sanskrit and German, for example, belong to the same language group, as had been realized in the mid-19th century. The deities invoked by the Nazis were mostly drawn from Nordic mythology, and so were very distantly related to the gods of the *Vedas*. The Nazis adopted the swastika as their own emblem and, where their stormtroopers went, the swastika, the redrawn symbol of the victorious Aryan sun-god, followed. The word swastika comes originally from the Sanskrit *svastika* meaning "good luck" or "well-being".

Warrior gods

Aryan gods are usually characterized as heroic warriors, representing the solar light of truth in the struggle against the powers of darkness. Verses in the *Rigveda* (see pp.16–17) praise Savitri, the deity who excites or stimulates action, the charioteer of a "golden car" that is pulled by "two bright steeds", who "banishes disease" and "directs the sun" on its victorious course. However, there may be other influences at work in Aryan mythology, and the gods of the *Vedas* may owe as much to the traditions of western Asia as to those of their homeland.

The first Aryans to enter the Indus Valley worshipped the deity Varuna, whose name is possibly derived from the Sanskrit verb *vri*, to cover, and it was as the encompasser or sovereign of the universe that he was best known. Varuna was upholder of the cosmic order, *rita*, a concept that shares many characteristics with that of other religions: the Sumerian principle of *me* or the Egyptian *maat* meaning justice, truth and harmony. Like the Yahweh of the Old Testament or the Sumerian deity Anu, Varuna was a wrathful god who was greatly feared. But he also offered mercy to those who worshipped him.

Varuna surpassed the other gods of the early Aryans as a moral ruler. Cosmic law was believed to work below as well as above the human realm. Just as the planets follow a fixed course on their journey through the heavens, so

This 19th-century engraving depicts Indra, armed with swords, riding his elephant, Airavata.

the Aryans believed that a "right" path must exist in the sphere of moral action. This notion of *rita* has parallels in Sumerian mathematics and astronomy. Pre-Aryan peoples like the Dravidians may also have influenced Vedic religion in ways which are no longer apparent.

Varuna appears to have been superseded by Indra as king of the Vedic gods. Indra was not so much a sovereign as a hero, and whereas Varuna was moody and vengeful, Indra was constant and strong. His most heralded act was his victory over Vritra, at first seen as a symbol of chaos, ignorance and darkness. Indra was a champion more in the mould of the warrior Aryans, who were alien to what remained of the Indus Valley culture's urban atmosphere.

In the 11th-century temple at Bhubaneshwar, eastern India, Varuna stands on the makara, *an aquatic monster, indicating his role as lord of the cosmic waters.*

The battle between Indra and the later gods of Hinduism, here represented by Krishna, is illustrated in this miniature painting from a late 16th-century manuscript. Indra can be seen riding his elephant. Krishna is depicted with his characteristic blue skin, as he rides through the clouds on the magical eagle Garuda. The four-headed Brahma and the ascetic Shiva are seated at the top of the painting.

INDRA AND VRITRA

Indra's slaying of the *brahmin* or, in early texts, the giant demon Vritra, is perhaps the most famous myth in the *Rigveda*. Vritra's name is thought by most scholars to be derived from the verb *ver*, meaning to speak the truth. Some commentators believe that Vritra represents the older cyclical cosmic order championed by Varuna. Indra, renowned for his awesome power, increases his strength still further by draining a vessel of the intoxicating drink *soma*. He launches a thunderbolt at Vritra, freeing the waters and setting the sun back onto its path. Words denoting strength and might were most often used to describe Indra, the ultimate warrior god, and prodigious drinker of *soma*.

But pre-Aryan India was not so easily eliminated. The great texts of Hinduism that were written 1,000 years later probably owe as much to indigenous Dravidian beliefs as they do to Aryan beliefs.

Like many later invaders of India, the Aryans were eventually assimilated and partly absorbed. Although modern Hindus claim the *Vedas* (see pp.16–17) as the source of their religion, what are probably pre-Aryan practices and beliefs, such as yoga and cyclical myths, became characteristic of later Hinduism.

The *Mahabharata* (see pp.56–7) depicts Vritra not as a demon but as a *brahmin* who has won his powers by asceticism. Indra is humbled by his power. Shiva advises him that only through even greater ascetic disciplines will he be able to slay Vritra – a new and very different approach from the Aryan conquering hero's.

The Vedas

An 18th-century manuscript of the Rigveda *("Wisdom of the Verses"), the earliest and most auspicious of the four* Vedas.

Despite their invincibility in battle, the greatest achievement of the Aryan invaders of India was the composition of the *Vedas* ("Books of Knowledge"). This collection of hymns and ritual incantations, known as *mantras* (see pp.98–99), was sung during sacrifices to the pantheon of Aryan gods. Although eclipsed by later teachings, the *Vedas* remain a central part of Hindu life to this day.

There are four *Vedas*: the first, the *Rigveda*, was composed before 1200BC, followed by the *Samaveda* and the *Yajurveda* and finally the *Atharvaveda,* which was probably written at a much later date. Each *Veda* is composed of two parts: the *Samhita,* in which the hymns or *mantras* are recited, and the *Brahmanas* which contain commentaries. The *Vedas* were composed for the different kinds of *brahmin* priest involved in a sacrifice: *hotri,* who officiated at sacrifices and recited the *mantras* of the *Rigveda*; *udgatri,* who sang the chants of the *Samaveda*; *adhvaryu,* who carried out sacrifices, chanting incantations from the *Yajurveda;* and *brahmin* overseers, who sang the *Atharvaveda*. Non-*brahmins* were denied access to the *Vedas.*

The *Vedas* are remarkable for the fact that both their origins and perpetuation were purely oral. Hindus believe not only the contents, but also the very sounds of the words to be sacred. The *brahmins* have passed the *Vedas* orally from generation to generation to the present day. Modern *brahmin* surnames such as Trivedi and Chaturvedi indicate early priestly roles. Hindus believe that the *Vedas* were revealed or "heard" (*srutri*), not composed by human beings, and that the power of the gods lies in these revealed words. Because they contain the sacred syllables from which gods and mortals were born, the *Vedas* are thought to have preceded the universe, itself created from the sacred syllable *Om* (see pp.108–9).

THE RIGVEDA

The *Rigveda* ("Wisdom of the Verses") is markedly polytheistic. It contains 1,028 hymns dedicated to thirty-three different gods, but mostly to Indra, Agni and Soma (see pp.18–19). The 10,589 verses of the *Rigveda* are divided into ten *mandalas* or books, of which books two to seven are the core of the work; the others appear to have been added at a later date. The traditional belief that each book was composed by seers, or *rishis*, of the same family seems to be born out by the particular metre, structure and poetic style that each contains. The books are arranged according to the number of hymns they possess. The main ritual referred to is sacrifice, the *brahmin* priests' main concern.

THE SAMAVEDA

The *Samaveda* ("Wisdom of the Chants") is better known for the intricacy and metre of its poetry than for its literary content. As sacrifice became an increasingly complex ritual in Vedic India, so the functions of the ever-growing body of *brahmin* priests had to be demarcated and defined. The *Samaveda* is a collection of *samans* or chants, drawn mainly from the eighth and ninth books of the *Rigveda*, for the *udgatri* priests who officiated at the *soma* sacrifice (see p.18). The *Samaveda* is more a collection of songs than *mantras*, and it includes precise instructions on how its verses should be sung.

THE YAJURVEDA

Yajurs are sacred formulas, invocations and spells muttered by the *adhvaryu* priests who performed the sacrificial rites, so the *Yajurveda* is called the "Wisdom of the Sacrifices". Although a few hymns to the gods are included in this text, it is more concerned with the actual mechanics of ritual. It involves invocations to the sacrificial instruments themselves which were believed to symbolize aspects of *brahman*, the Hindu concept of godhead.

THE ATHARVAVEDA

The *Atharvaveda* ("Wisdom of the Atharvan Priests") takes its name from one of the *brahmin* families traditionally believed to have composed the *Vedas*. Like the *Rigveda*, it is a collection of entire hymns, but its lack of connection with Vedic ritual sacrifice has persuaded many that it was compiled at a much later date than the other three. It is primarily a book of spells for everything from success in love to the realization of other worldly ambitions.

THE HORSE SACRIFICE

The most elaborate of all Vedic rituals was the Horse Sacrifice. One year passed between the choosing of the stallion and its eventual slaughter. The sacrifice was usually ordered by a king. Both the stallion and the king had to remain celibate for the year, during which time the horse could wander freely, escorted by the king's men. If the stallion crossed the border of an adjacent kingdom, the ruler of that kingdom had the choice either of war or of accepting the overlordship of his neighbour. On the appointed day, the stallion was led to the city and presented with a mare. The point at which the horse neighed in joy was the moment at which he was suffocated.

This 17th-century image of a horse adorns the temple tower of a shrine to the god Ayyappan in Tamil Nadu. Horses were symbols of Aryan power, pulling the chariots in which they invaded India.

Gods of the sacrifice

Sacrifice was the central rite of the Vedic tradition, the sacred medium through which the Aryans invoked and appeased the gods. The sacrifice was a symbol of the creation of the world, with the sacrificer assuming the role of the first man who sacrificed himself so that the universe could be born.

All ritual acts in the sacrifice were performed by *brahmin* priests, who numbered as many as seventeen in the full *soma* ceremony. Instructions for the correct performance of the sacrifice were outlined in the *Brahmanas*, a series of lengthy prose commentaries attached to each of the *Vedas*. They advised that an area should first be sanctified by the *brahmins*, and that the householder who had sponsored the sacrifice should be ritually set apart. The altar was said to represent earth and water, the basic elements from which the world was created.

The consecrated sacrificial area came to represent a sphere of purity in what the *brahmins* considered to be an impure world, and the later *Brahmanas* displayed a growing aversion to the killing of sacrificial objects. Animals were killed by suffocation, outside the sanctified arena, but in later times were replaced by symbolic substitutes.

SOMA

The god Soma represents liquid, coolness and the moon. He is the "draught of immortality", the sacrificial meal on which the gods feed. Soma is the personification of a hallucinogenic plant, the preparation of which lay at the heart of Vedic sacrifice.

There is much debate as to the identity of the *soma* plant that was pressed and drunk during sacrifice. Many believe it to be the hallucinogenic mushroom *Amanita muscaria*, commonly known as the fly agaric. The property of *soma*, the "elixir of the gods", that is most often discussed is the sense of euphoria and ecstasy experienced by those who drink it. *Soma*, like the fly agaric, is thought to have been red. It is supposed to have been pressed and bottled before it could be drunk. In the *Rigveda*, *soma* is often called *madhu* (honey) and *pavamana* (a tawny yellowish liquid), possibly referring to the dark yellow colour of the mushroom after it has been pressed.

Amanita muscaria has been used for thousands of years by Siberian shamans to induce ecstatic states. The plant grows in Siberia and Afghanistan and would have been familiar to the Aryans in their original homeland. However, supplies in the Indus Valley and northern plains of India would have been minimal, and it seems that the Aryans' decreasing contact with the fly agaric

The hallucinogenic mushroom, Amanita muscaria.

was met by an increasing elaboration of the *soma* ritual. The mushroom was probably replaced by another substance and, eventually, it was perhaps the ritual itself, filled with magic formulae and sacred syllables, that induced the ecstatic state described in the *Vedas*.

RUDRA

One of the most interesting of the Vedic deities is Rudra, the "howler", a storm god who wields the thunderbolt as his weapon of destruction. Rudra is the most angry of the Aryan gods. He inhabits the wilds, and is filthy, with matted hair, a black belly and a red back. His wrath is infinite and unprovoked, but unlike the warriors Indra and Varuna, he does not fight on the side of the gods in their battles. Food is not offered to him in sacrifice but is thrown to the ground in a ball, in the same ritual through which local spirits are appeased. Rudra is generally believed to be a prototype of Shiva (see pp.74–5), Lord of Yoga and Destruction, since the epithet "*shiva*" or auspicious is often used to describe him in the *Vedas*.

Agni, god of fire, shown riding a goat, in a miniature painting from an 18th-century watercolour album produced for European visitors.

AGNI

More than 200 of the hymns in the *Rigveda* are dedicated to Agni, god of fire. As a deity representing the forces of light he is often associated with Indra, god of the sun (see p.15) and, like the king of the gods, he is invincible in battle, burning his enemies to ashes when they oppose him. He is the lord of the cremation ground and of the forest fire; his is the "heat" (*tapas*) generated by yogic austerities.

Agni's birth is variously described. On earth his parents are the two sticks from which fire is made, everyoung because the fire is kindled daily. He appears in the world of humans as lightning in the sky, as the fire of the stomach that "heats" or digests food, and in the hearth that is the centre of every home.

Agni's most important role is to manifest himself as the fire that burns upon the sacrificial altar. He burns the demons who threaten to destroy the sacrifice, and summons the gods from the heavens to participate in the ritual. Finally, he carries the sacrifice to them so that they can eat the offerings. He is therefore often depicted riding a goat, the sacrificial animal, or wearing a goat's head with flames behind it.

Because he embodies the sacrifice, Agni is believed to be the mediator between gods and mortals, the divine priest who understands both the ways of the earth and of the heavens.

The mother goddess

The mother goddess in India is a figure of great antiquity that has survived through the ages in a multitude of guises. Essentially, she both provides and destroys. She is the broad-hipped womb of life from which the burgeoning abundance of the jungle flows. She is the "dark one" with the "long red tongue", garlanded by skulls, who wantonly takes back the life she has granted to her mortal offspring. Her image has endured the many incarnations of Hinduism: today she can be seen in the deities Durga and Kali (see pp.80–81), ferocious destroyers of ignorance and illusion, as well as in the more benign image of Parvati, beloved consort of the god Shiva (see pp.74–5).

At the core of mother goddess worship is the vegetal-lunar mythology of life, death and endless return. Like the moon which dies every month only to be reborn, the plants and animals of the jungle are continually born into a brief and danger-filled life, feeding from the death of others before they too must die. The basic myth of rejuvenation is of a divine male being who is murdered, sliced up and planted in a village grove; it is from this grove that the food of the world is said to have grown. The murder also results in the appearance of sexual organs when the food is eaten. Sex and the differentiation of woman and man are thus said to have emerged as a result of this event. The two faces of the mother goddess, sex and death, are the two principles on which the ever-revolving wheel of life depends.

The ritual that invariably lay at the heart of mother-goddess worship was sacrifice. To this day at the Kalighat festival in Calcutta, up to 800 goats are slaughtered, their heads piled before the image of the goddess Kali, and throughout rural India, animals are sacrificed to satisfy her insatiable appetite. Human sacrifice was outlawed as recently as 1835, and several accounts written up to that date depict a village culture in which it thrived. The Aryan "seers" abstracted and symbolized the sacrifice, so that eventually the elaborate language and ceremony of the *brahmin* priests became as significant as the killing itself.

The origins of the mother goddess, and of the animal and human sacrifices that attended the rites with which she was worshipped, can be traced back to an era that precedes the arrival of the Aryans. Terracotta figurines dating from the 3rd and 2nd millennia BC, found at various sites across India, show females with prominent breasts and exaggerated hips. Their highly elaborate headdresses and jewelry suggest that they may have been cult figures who would have been worshipped as goddesses – precursors of the powerful representation of womanhood which has been in existence through the centuries, and which is still in evidence in India today.

Terracotta figurines, c.2000 BC, found in the Indus Valley, show richly dressed females who are believed to be mother goddesses.

RIGHT *Kali, goddess of destruction, revered today throughout India, is the subject of this 19th-century painting from Calcutta.*

BELOW *Festivals which celebrate female divinities continue to be a common feature of religious life in India. Here a priest officiates before a ten-armed goddess.*

THE SPIRIT OF THE TREE

Many elements of mother-goddess worship are derived from the animistic beliefs that characterized pre-Aryan religions in India and are still found among India's tribal populations today. Just as natural features such as rivers, mountains and trees were believed to be possessed by animating spirits, so the earth itself was thought to represent the body of the mother goddess. Banyan trees (see right) are especially revered as symbols of nature's abundance and are said to be possessed by Shalabhanjika, the goddess of trees. Beads made from the seeds of banyan trees are worn in honour of both the mother goddess and Shiva.

The Upanishads

The *Upanishads* is a collection of texts that were composed mainly between the 7th and 5th centuries BC. They form the last part of the *Vedas* (see pp.16–17), the sacred texts of the Aryans, and are called the *Vedanta* ("Conclusion of the *Veda*"). They are, nevertheless, very different in content and tone from the earlier *Vedas*. In the *Upanishads*, philosophical and mystical questionings replace earlier Vedic concerns with ritual sacrifice. The *Upanishads'* 108 texts are central to later Hinduism, and have attracted many commentaries.

By 500 BC both religion and society in India were changing rapidly. The swift growth of cities, with the subsequent emergence of a strong merchant class, meant that the old *varnas* (orders: priest, warrior, trader and serf) no longer corresponded so neatly with reality. Breakaway sects of ascetics, mystics and renunciants repudiated the authority of the *brahmin* priests and their long-established monopoly of religion. Instead, they followed teachers such as Siddhartha Gautama, who became the Buddha (see pp.30–35), and Vardhamana, who became Mahavira (see pp.40–43). This led to a transformation of Indian religious life.

More than any other Hindu text, the *Upanishads* embody this transformation. Rather than invoking external gods, the *Upanishads* look for a god within, so that the emphasis shifts from ritualized acts of sacrifice to the search for the sacred force (*brahman*) that lives in all things. Just as the Aryan sages believed that the sacrifice embodied and mirrored the divine, so the emerging new philosophy saw *brahman's*

with the divine was no longer to be achieved through external ritual but by an inward transformation.

The outer trappings of divine worship, which were so important to later Vedic religion and could involve the sacrifice of scores of animals, were not only avoided but were vehemently rejected. Well before 700 BC, Indian sages were chanting *neti neti* (not that, not that), denying the ultimate reality of an external world in which they saw little more than illusion, and searching instead for the eternal spark of *brahman* in the soul within all beings. The prime concern of most of the *Upanishads* is the desire for release (*moksha*) from transmigration, a concept by then almost universally accepted by those familiar with the sacred texts. This was to be gained through meditation, yoga and asceticism, to unite the *atman*

This handwritten page of Sanskrit text is from manuscript of the Chandogya Upanishad. *Originally composed between the 8th and 7th centuries* BC, *the* Chandogya *is one of the oldest* Upanishads *and is best known for its equation of the* atman *(soul) within, with the* brahman *(absolute spirit) without.*

BALAKI AND KING JABALI

The teachings contained in the *Upanishads* were no longer the exclusive property of the *brahmin* priests, as the *Vedas* had been, but could be followed by the *kshatriyas* (see p.25), the class of kings and warriors from which the Buddha came, and whose prestige now often eclipsed the *brahmins*'.

The earliest, and thus the least mystical or philosophical *Upanishad*, tells the story of Balaki, a proud and learned *brahmin* who approached the king of Benares to instruct him in the *Vedas*. The king offered

the *brahmin* 1,000 cows if he could reveal to him the nature of *brahman* (absolute spirit). The priest first displayed the sun, then the moon, the elements, lightning, thunder and *soma* – all symbols of the Vedic gods – but the king was not satisfied. Instead, he himself expounded the theory of *atman* (soul), yoga and the cycle of rebirth to the humbled *brahmin*.

A variant on the same mythic tale concerns a *brahmin* who sent his son to the palace of King Jabali. The king asked the boy if his father had instructed him in religion. The *brahmin's* son replied that he had, and was

questioned by the king about what happens to creatures when they die and how their souls return. The boy was unable to answer the king's questions and returned to his father in shame. The *brahmin* himself came before the king and asked for the knowledge that he lacked. The king's answer exposed the meaning of caste, *karma* (see pp.24–5), yoga and rebirth, which are the basis of much of later Hindu theory.

Another *Upanishad*, dated *c.*600BC, carried this radical notion further by subordinating the Vedic deities to the mother goddess, who alone is able to recognize *brahman*.

Karma

The law of *karma* states that just as every action has a cause, so actions have reactions that are impossible to escape. *Karma* is the cause of our particular destiny, the law of nature that ensures that we become what we think or do. Misfortunes in our present life are the result of acts that we have committed in the past. Suicide, according to the law of *karma*, is not therefore an option: *karma* cannot be escaped or deferred and its effects will only be worse if we try to avoid it.

Our actions in our present lives determine our fate in the lives that follow, and consciousness itself is believed to be a *karmic* memory, contained by *vijnana*, the higher conscious mind, throughout the many incarnations of *atman*, the soul. Desire is the cause of *karma*, and it is because we still have desires to operate in the realm of action, to live normal lives in the world, that we are constantly reborn into the cycle of *samsara*, the endless chain of reincarnation.

According to Krishna, Arjuna's charioteer in the *Bhagavad Gita* (see pp.60–61), the soul assumes bodies, or sheaths, as long as it still yearns to live and act, "just as a man discards an old garment and puts on one that is new". The traditions of forest philosophy (see pp.38–9) maintained that only by completely renouncing action and the external illusion of the world can we be free of *karma*, and thus find *moksha*, or release from reincarnation.

In the *Bhagavad Gita*, however, Krishna teaches that our actions need not necessarily produce a negative *karmic* result if we act disinterestedly, so that we are unconcerned about

the fruits or rewards of our deeds. Disciplined action, according to Krishna, is the way of truth (*dharma*) and the path to *brahman* (the godhead). By offering our every action, thought and word to *brahman,* the ill effects of *karma* are nullified and the *atman* (the soul) is free of egotistical desire.

Dharma is the basis of the modern Hindu religion. Hinduism is known as *Sanatana Dharma*, the eternal or universal *dharma*, and *dharma* is considered to be the mainstay of all things, the most basic law of the universe manifested in the cosmic order and in the rightful action of humanity. It is a fundamental moral code, the way that we should act in accordance with our own

Karma *literally means action. In the* Bhagavad Gita, *Krishna recognizes it as one of the three paths that lead to self-realization and release. The first is* jnana *(knowledge), the second* bhakti *(devotion), and the third* karma – *the way of work or activity. For Krishna, work is superior to renunciation as a path to release because "Not by leaving works undone, does a man win freedom…nor by renunciation alone can he win perfection." This positive approach balances the ascetics' renunciant tendencies.*

karma. The *brahmin* has his own particular *dharma*, as do the *kshatriya*, *vaishya* and *shudra* groups. Action without desire, according to Krishna, is action with *dharma*, drawing us nearer to our higher consciousness. "Whatever causes devotion to me to increase…" says Krishna "…that is *dharma*."

CASTES

Since Vedic times, the Indian theory of society has been based on a classification into four main groups called *varnas*, literally "colour". Within each *varna* there are numerous groups called *jati*. Each *jati* traditionally carried out a specialized occupation such as pottery, weaving or farming. Both the *varnas* and the *jatis* within them are classified into higher and lower, though the detailed order is often a matter of dispute. The Portuguese called these *jatis* castes, meaning "pure" groups.

The **brahmin** *varna* is the highest, because of the ritual purity associated with the main *brahmin* occupation as priest of the gods. Today, not all *brahmins* are priests, but most are still vegetarian and observe practices such as frequent bathing and (for men) the wearing of a sacred thread received in a special rite at adolescence.

The **kshatriya** or warrior *varna* contains several castes. These were traditionally kings or nobles, but also included scribes and other court officials.

The third *varna* are the **vaishya** traditionally farmers and merchants.

The fourth *varna*, the **shudra,** traditionally performed labouring occupations.

Below the four *varnas* are the **harijans** or "children of god", as they were termed by Mahatama Gandhi. Lying in a sense outside the caste system, these are widely known as "untouchables", since their very contact can defile an orthodox member of a high caste. Their supposed uncleanliness is related to their impure occupations, such as sweeper or lavatory cleaner. In modern India the relationship between caste and class is complex. Although the constitution of independent India, which was drafted by the *harijan* lawyer Bhimrao Ambedkar, made the practice of untouchability illegal, in reality this has proved hard to enforce.

Renunciation

Before the middle of the 1st millennium BC,
the *brahmin* priests who performed the Vedic
sacrifices had a near monopoly of official
religious life and ritual in northern India. But
many, both *brahmins* and others, began to
feel that ritual sacrifice no longer satisfied all
their religious needs, and they started practising renunciation and self-denial. Rather than
honouring the sacrificial fire, growing numbers of wandering ascetics sought the "inner
heat" attained by fasting and meditation.
The Buddha and Mahavira, the founders of
Buddhism and Jainism respectively, drew
their followers from such renunciants, being
themselves renowned ascetics.

The ascetics' primary aim was to attain
"release" from the material world and from
the endless cycle of birth and death. Central
to this forest philosophy were the concepts of
samsara (rebirth) and *karma* (the belief that
past actions influence an individual's future
lives). The Jains believed that the only means
of escape from the binds of the material
world was by rigorous self-discipline and
non-violence.

The Buddha's "Middle Way" between
asceticism and materialism sought to eliminate suffering, and was the basis of an early
Buddhism that could be practised by laymen
as well as monks.

*Expelled from western India by invading Muslims in the 12th
century, and under pressure from brahmins, renunciant followers
of the Buddha and Mahavira were later mostly based in the
Ganges basin and the foothills of the eastern Himalayas, shown
here. Ascetic communities developed new kinds of worship, such
as inscribing the names of their gods on their prayer flags.*

Forest philosophies

deep into the forest where they gathered fruits and vegetables.

Central to the philosophy of these renunciants was the concept of "going forth" (*pravrajya*) from home. To avoid becoming attached to particular parts of the forest, they continually moved on, stopping only when monsoon rains made progress impossible. Some practised severe austerities in their search for *moksha* (release from physical ties), almost starving themselves to death, or experiencing extremes of heat and cold to attain mental control over their bodies. They were sometimes known as *shramanas* (strivers) because of the physical exertions required by their path.

One of the late hymns in the *Rigveda* (see pp.16–17) speaks of *munis*; wandering ascetics who practised meditation and asceticism as techniques to attain release by way of ecstasy. Both the Buddha (see pp.30–31) and the Jain teacher Mahavira (see pp.40–41) assumed roles that were comparable to the Vedic *munis*, spending parts of their lives as wandering ascetics. The forest philosophy of the Buddha, Mahavira

From the 8th century BC onward, ascetics who had renounced the world travelled the forests of northern India, forming groups from which the followers of Buddhism, Jainism and the Ajivikas later emerged. These wanderers rejected all ties with society, even breaking contact with their friends and family. They begged for food, or retired

and Goshala stressed internal sacrifice, and replaced the flames of the sacrificial fire with the inner heat (*tapas*) of contemplation and asceticism. Like sacrifice, asceticism was a quest to overcome the limitations of the manifest world. But unlike Vedic priests, these renunciants sought the power to do so by controlling their minds, since the mind controlled the body and its perception of the outer world.

The Upanishadic principles of *karma* and *samsara* had largely been accepted as basic facts of human existence by the 6th century BC. *Samsara* (flow) is the cycle of constant rebirth caused by the accumulation of one's actions (*karma*). Opposed to the ultimate reality experienced in searching for *moksha*, *samsara* refers to this world of illusion and suffering, in which everything is subject to constant change. One of the most important features of Jainism and the Ajivikas, and of Buddhism as it developed, was the acceptance of transmigration and therefore of the escape from rebirth as the primary goal. Since rebirth was believed to be caused by harmful action, it was by "right action" that the renunciants sought release, often rejecting the norms of social convention seen as *dharma* (morality).

AJIVIKAS

Ajivikas were a sect of ascetics that emerged at the same time as Buddhism. Their most famous saint, Maskarin Goshala, was an associate of Mahavira until they quarrelled. Most of what we know of Goshala's life comes from later Buddhist and Jain texts, and is coloured by their dislike of a rival sect which they thought heretical. They depict Goshala as a complete determinist, recognizing destiny or fate (*niyati*) as the sole important force in the universe. All human efforts to attain liberation are useless; appointed events – according to Goshala – are predestined and unavoidable.

FOREST COMMUNITIES

One of the most striking features of forest life was its degree of organization. The renunciants established groups whose social structure and regulation were strangely similar to that of the world that they had left behind. The sudden increase in their numbers in the 6th century BC is frequently explained by social and economic changes in contemporary northern India, where the aggressive empire-building of the Magadha dynasty was an increasing threat to the warlike tribal societies on its borders, in which both the Buddha and Mahavira were born. Buddhist and Jain terms such as *gana* (troop) and *sangha* (community) were commonly used in the *Vedas* to describe nomadic warrior brotherhoods, whose membership – like the forest orders – was governed by age, fitness and high birth.

This Vaishnavite ascetic has renounced all worldly ties to live in an ascetic sangha *(community) in the holy city of Puri.*

NAKED MONKS

Indian mysticism seldom travelled west, but when Alexander the Great reached northern India in 326BC, he wanted to meet Indian philosophers. He was led to a group of forest monks sitting naked on a rock, so hot that his soldiers could hardly step on it. Most of the monks refused to talk, but one of them, named Kalanos by the Greeks, left the rock to join Alexander's entourage. When the army arrived in Persia, Kalanos asked for a funeral pyre to be built and garlanded with flowers. He then assumed a seated yogic posture on the fire and immolated himself before a silent Greek army.

The life of the Buddha

A 5th-century AD mural at Ajanta, Maharashtra, depicting part of the Mahajanaka Jataka, *the story of one of the Buddha's former lives.*

The Buddha (the "Awakened One") was born as Siddhartha Gautama in *c*.563BC. He was an actual historical figure, a prince of the Shakyas, the people of a small state bordering modern India and Nepal. He lived in a time of prosperity and social upheaval. A road stretched from northern India to Greece, allowing ideas to be exchanged freely. The Buddha was roughly contemporary with the Greek philosophers Pythagoras and Heraclitus, and with Mahavira, the last of the Jain *Tirthankaras* (see p.40).

What is known of Gautama's life until he reached the age of twenty-nine, is largely mythological. Later Mahayana texts eulogized Siddhartha Gautama, portraying his life as a predestined path to Buddhahood. The king, his father, made every effort to keep the future Buddha from the hardship of his path, forcing him to remain within the palace grounds while providing him with every material luxury. At the age of sixteen, Siddhartha married a beautiful woman and they had a son, which fulfilled the basic duties of his role as the head of a traditional Indian household. The turning point came when Siddhartha was twenty-nine and he ventured outside the palace grounds.

Recognizing the auspiciousness of the moment, the gods rejoiced, sending "four signs" to earth that would awaken the future Buddha to his path. The first "sign" that he saw was an old man, decrepit and leaning on a stick. The future Buddha, until now protected from the reality of suffering in the outside world, asked his charioteer why the man was so weak. The charioteer answered that the man was old, and that old age afflicts all men. The future Buddha was greatly disturbed by this experience. When he went out the next

An urban procession, from a narrative of the Buddha's life on the 1st-century AD gateway to the stupa *at Sanchi in Madhya Pradesh.*

day he was shocked by the sight of a man riddled with disease. He enquired as to the cause, and was told that everyone suffers in the grasp of illness. On a third occasion, he saw a corpse being carried to cremation, and so discovered that death was in the world.

Old age, sickness and death became known as the "three marks of impermanence". They revealed that due to its absolute transience, life is indivisible from suffering (*dukkha*). Racked with doubt, the future Buddha once more went forth from the palace. One of the gods appeared before him as a wandering holy man, whose tranquillity persuaded the prince that contemplation offered the possibility of release from the suffering that he saw at the heart of existence. Soon after, Siddhartha left his wife and child and set out dressed as a wandering ascetic.

Beginning his search for enlightenment, the future Buddha went south, in the direction of the central areas of spiritual learning. After instruction from the most distinguished gurus, he arrived at a forest hermitage. The naked monks, who practised severe austerities, taught that pain and denial were the source of release. Siddhartha denied this, arguing that since it is through the mind that the body functions, it is the mind, not the body, that should be under complete control. He therefore rejected the path of asceticism and continued his search for enlightenment.

At the age of thirty-five, Gautama finally arrived at Bodh Gaya, where he sat beneath a tree that has subsequently been interpreted as the Tree of Life (see pp.33). He swore that he would not rise until he had found enlightenment. After forty-nine days of solitary meditation he attained *nirvana*, the state of permanence that lies within the flux of daily life. He thus became the Buddha, "One Who is Fully Awake".

THE FASTING BUDDHA

Siddhartha met five ascetics who practised extreme austerities in their search for truth. Persuading the prince of the need to mortify the body, they sat together to fast. The future Buddha refused food until his navel touched his spine. Many images depict him in this emaciated state. He surmised from this experience that the body needs energy in order to fuel the mind's quest for enlightenment, and he later abandoned such extremes of renunciation.

A 3rd-century AD schist image of the future Buddha, emaciated from fasting, from Gandhara, Pakistan.

The Buddha's enlightenment

The empty throne beneath the tree in this 1st-century AD relief, at the Sanchi Bhopal temple, symbolizes the enlightenment of the Buddha.

The story of the Buddha's enlightenment is central to the whole of Buddhism, in both its Hinayana and Mahayana forms (see pp.38–9). Siddhartha had spent six years practising extreme austerities which left him emaciated before he realized that such a path was leading him nowhere. He began to eat normally again and so broke with the fasting monks, who had hailed him as their leader. The future Buddha, Siddhartha Gautama, then approached a tree at a site now known as Bodh Gaya ("the place of enlightenment"), beneath which he sat cross-legged, facing the rising sun. He vowed that he would not move until he had gained enlightenment.

In an episode resembling later Biblical accounts of Christ's temptation in the wilderness, the future Buddha was approached by Mara, the Lord of Death, with his sons Confusion, Gaiety and Pride, and his daughters Lust, Delight and Pining. All entreated Siddhartha to abandon his goal, reminding him of his caste duty as a king (*kshatriya*) and of his opportunities for wealth and fame. Siddhartha remained impassive, with his eyes closed to the outer world.

Mara then took up his bow with its arrows of temptation – Exciter, Gladdener, Infatuator, Parcher and Bringer of Death – and fired an arrow at the holy man. But the arrow could not harm Siddhartha, for he had completely dissolved his temporal identity, and there was no self that could be tempted or terrified by the Lord of

MUCHILINDA

After gaining enlightenment the Buddha sat under a *muchilinda* tree for seven days, enjoying the bliss of enlightenment. A terrible storm broke out while he sat oblivious, but the *naga* (serpent) king Muchilinda emerged from his lair and wrapped the sage in seven coils of his body, stretching his hood over the Buddha like an umbrella. The myth suggests the basic unity of the universe: enlightenment is for all creatures.

Death's words. Mara finally threw the force of his terrible armies against his foe. Many-headed demons raged, while naked women carrying skulls flitted distractingly before his eyes. The gods in the heavens fled in panic and the future Buddha was left alone. Mara then sent great winds but not even the hem of Siddhartha's robe was moved; rocks and awesome weapons were turned into flowers by the power of his meditation, and the Lord of Death's darkness dissolved "as night does at dawn". Mara, beaten, disappeared.

In the first "watch" of that night, Siddhartha acquired total knowledge of his previous births. Thinking to himself that "all existence whatsoever is insubstantial" he came to a profound understanding of the need for compassion (*karuna*), since all beings are caught in an endless cycle of suffering and rebirth (*samsara*). During the second part of the night, he gained divine sight, perceiving a chain of causality which leads to rebirth, and is therefore at root of suffering (*dukkha*).

Finally, in the the last part of the night, the future Buddha came fully to understand the workings of *karma*, and graduated through the eight stages of meditation (*dhyana*) that led him to Perfection. At that moment, the Buddha – now fully awake – reached enlightenment, attaining total spiritual insight. In recognition of this momentous spiritual event, nature itself responded and the "ten thousand worlds" (of the cosmos) thundered and shook in celebration. Garlands of flowers rained down from the heavens, for humankind now had hope of release from the endless cycle of suffering, birth and death.

Again Mara came to tempt him. He entreated the now-enlightened Buddha to enjoy his own enlightenment in the heavenly realms of *nirvana* (literally, "snuffing" or "blowing out"; the extinction of the self), far from the tedious task of preaching. Overcoming his fears that no one would understand his teachings, he set off to teach his Noble Eight-fold Path.

BODH GAYA

The Tree of Life is an almost universal archetype in the myths and legends of the world. In Christianity it is represented as both the fateful Tree of Knowledge and as Jacob's Ladder. In Nordic myth, Ygdrasil is the giant ash tree supporting the universe, while in Buddhism the Tree of Life appears as Bodh Gaya, the sacred tree under which the Buddha gained enlightenment. The tree represents the hub that remains stationary in the middle of the ever-revolving wheel of time, life and death.

A statue of the meditating Buddha in the shrine at Bodh Gaya, site of the sacred bodhi *tree, beneath which the Master sat and vowed not to move until he had attained enlightenment.*

The sermons of the Buddha

Various depictions of the Buddha from the 5th-century painted sanctuaries at Ajanta in Maharashtra.

After his enlightenment at the age of thirty-five, the Buddha travelled around northern India for forty-five years, teaching his Middle Way to growing numbers of disciples. Although insisting on his teachings as the only truth, the Buddha asked that his followers should never idolize him. He preached the need for enlightenment and an end to suffering and ignorance, claiming that his solution was the only one.

The Buddha's teachings were logical rather than dogmatic in nature, and he encouraged his disciples to find solutions based on their own experiences. He criticized caste distinctions and the role of the *brahmins* (the priestly caste). The *Dhammapada* (a Pali poem about *dharma*, teaching) ascribes to him the words: "A man does not become a *brahmin* by long hair, or by family, or by birth. The man in whom there is truth and holiness is filled with joy and he is a *brahmin*." Although the Buddha himself worshipped no gods, he did not condemn their worship but questioned unthinking acceptance of gods if they did not lead to the relief of suffering.

The first sermon, known as *The First Turning of the Wheel of Law*, was delivered by the Buddha at the Deer Park in Sarnath, near Varanasi, to his disciples, the five ascetics with whom he had fasted before he attained enlightenment (see p.31). The Sarnath sermon is based upon the Four Noble Truths: life is rooted in suffering (*dukkha*); suffering is caused by craving (*tanha*) for power, pleasure and long life; by eliminating this craving there is release from suffering and so the chance to achieve *nirvana*; the way to eliminate craving and thus suffering is to follow the Noble Eight-fold Path.

Dukkha is usually translated as suffering, which includes the concepts of impermanence and imperfection. Life is *dukkha*, as there are always the "three marks of impermanence" first encountered by the Buddha as a young man (see pp.30–31): old age, sickness and death. We suffer because we crave permanence in our current lives and in our after-lives, but the Buddha taught that nothing is permanent. Life is not inherently sorrowful, but its impermanence makes it imperfect and unsatisfactory to humans.

The root of craving is *avidya*, a false concept of the nature of reality. The Buddha proclaimed the doctrine of *anatta* (not-self), denying the existence of a permanent soul or self. He deemed identification with the self to be the cause of much human suffering. Many of his teachings offer, via meditation, practical methods for his followers to free themselves from the delusion of the supremacy of the self.

THE NOBLE EIGHT-FOLD PATH

The Noble Eight-fold Path is at the heart of daily Buddhist practice. It is not a ritual that can only be performed by an elite priesthood, but a way of life and practical guide available to all. The Eight-fold Path is based on eight principles that are inter-related. These principles are repeated in the same order, with only one occasional variation. They are: right understanding, right intention, right speech, right action, right livelihood, right effort, right awareness and right concentration (*samadi*). The reward for following the Eight-fold Path is the attainment of *nirvana*, which the Buddha promised was available to humans in the last of his Four Noble Truths.

THE MIDDLE WAY

The Buddha's path to enlightenment, The Middle Way, is midway between the extremes of luxury and asceticism. He was brought up as a prince, completely protected from the cruelties of life, but later joined a group of monks fasting and practising other austerities.

The Buddha preaching to his disciples amidst lakes, forests and mountains, from an 18th-century painting.

FLOWER SERMON

The "Flower Sermon" greatly inspired Zen Buddhism as it developed in Japan. When asked to define enlightenment by his disciples, the Buddha remained silent and simply held up a flower. He taught that words stand for objects and ideas that are familiar to us and can be expressed. Truth and Enlightenment are beyond our understanding.

This 5th-century icon of the Buddha, from Mathura in central India, shows the Awakened One seated on a throne, one hand held up in the "fear not" mudra (hand gesture). Mudras were one of the major symbolic means of conveying key principles of Buddhist thought.

Stupas

The magnificent entrance portal to the 2nd-century BC stupa at Sanchi in eastern India.

The rigours of the Indian climate and the predominant use of wood as a building material mean that we have little idea of the nature of Indian religious art and architecture prior to the early centuries of the 1st millennium AD. However, the cave-temples carved from rock after the 2nd century BC are remarkable for their scale and intricacy. The earliest surviving stone buildings are probably the Buddhist *stupas* (commemorative burial mounds). These increasingly intricate structures, often adorned with sculptures, dominated Buddhist art until about the 7th century AD when Buddhism was largely displaced by Hinduism as the religion of the ruling dynasties.

The first *stupas* were built by the emperor Ashoka, who converted to Buddhism in the 3rd century BC. With the zeal of a new convert, Ashoka is said to have constructed *stupas* throughout the domains of his fast-

SYMBOL OF THE STUPA

Early Buddhist artists represented the Buddha symbolically, using legends of his past and present lives as subjects for their works. The base of a *stupa* was decorated with elaborate reliefs showing the teeming life of earthly existence. It formed a symbolic foundation over which the domed burial mound was built, entombing the remains. The two structures were joined by a central mast representing the tree at Bodh Gaya, under which Buddha attained enlightenment (see pp.32–3).

A square balcony at the summit of the dome indicated the heaven of the thirty-three gods. Each was sheltered by umbrellas, pre-Buddhist symbols of royalty.

The earliest *stupas* were intended as monuments in

The eyes of the Buddha overlook the stupas in Nepal and gaze out in four directions from the mast above the dome.

praise of the Lord Buddha, but they later embodied symbolic significance as representations of the Three Jewels (*triratna*): the Buddha, the Law (*dharma*) and the Community of Monks (*sangha*).

expanding Mauryan empire. The dome-shaped monuments are believed to symbolize the Buddhist path to liberation and to house the bodily relics of the Buddha and his prominent disciples.

Ashoka is reported to have built anything between 1,000 and 84,000 *stupas*, although none has survived, with the possible exception of one at Bhilsa. Of the *stupas* remaining from this period, the Great Stupa at Sanchi in eastern India is probably the finest example. Much of what we know about the use of wood in early Indian architecture comes from the study of the "imitative art" that decorates the portals forming entrances to the Great Stupa, as stone-masons copied the designs used in local wooden structures that have since per-ished. Events from the Buddha's past lives are depicted in a series of panels on the posts and lintels of Sanchi's portals, and were intended to be viewed in sequence. The Buddha himself, however, is only represented indirectly, by empty thrones, footprints and emblematic forms such as the wheel.

The vigour and sense of movement of these carvings may have inspired the more elaborate Buddhist art of the Gupta and Pala dynasties, from the 4th to the 8th centuries AD. Contrary to earlier representations, the Buddha was now depicted in human form as Shakyamuni, the historical prince who found his own enlightenment and who preached the doctrines which became the basis of the new religion.

BUDDHIST CAVE-TEMPLES

Cave-temples were built by forcing wooden pegs into holes bored into a cliff face. When the pegs were moistened they expanded, splitting the rock into manageable blocks which were then removed with picks and bars. Sections of stone were left in place either to form false pillars in imitation of the supporting pillars of wooden temples, or to act as blocks which would be fashioned into sculptures, as in Buddhist cave-temples.

Sculptures in the 5th-century caves at Ajanta, western India, show Buddha teaching (right), and lying lifeless on his side in the "Great Decease" (above).

Mahayana and Theravada Buddhism

This image from a 19th-century mural, depicting a branch of the sacred bodhi *tree being shipped from India in a Great Ferry, symbolizes the spread of Mahayana Buddhism.*

the contemplative and devotional strands of Indian religion and, like the popularized forms of Hinduism that developed during the same era, it places love and compassion on equal terms with knowledge as a means to enlightenment.

Whereas the schools of the Theravadins stressed the importance of monastic life and austerity, excluding the possibility of a lay person from attaining liberation, the Mahayanists claimed that enlightenment was open to all who followed the path of devotion and contemplation, whatever their status in life.

Theravada Buddhism honoured the historical figure of Siddhartha Gautama as the sole Buddha and the only holder of the Truth. The Mahayanists looked beyond his material form, and represented the Buddha as a transcendent godhead of which the historical figure, the Gautama Buddha, was but one of many earthly manifestations.

Compassion is the key concept of the Mahayana. It is found in the fervent devotionalism practised by Mahayana

Mahayana (Greater Ferry) Buddhism emerged at the end of the first millennium BC as a reaction against the more sober schools of Buddhism represented by the Theravadins. The latter schools were termed Hinayana (Lesser Ferry) Buddhism by the Mahayanists.

Mahayana is the most widely practised form of Buddhism in China, Tibet, Japan and Korea. Mahayana Buddhism is said to be a synthesis of

BUDDHAS AND BODHISATTVAS

In common with the gods of devotionalist Hinduism, a vast body of myth surrounded the Mahayana Bodhisattvas and Buddhas. The historical Buddha was worshipped as one of several "celestial" Buddhas, such as Amitabha, creator of the Pure Buddha-Realm in the West. He is said to have attained Buddhahood when he swore that he would reject it unless it enabled him to come to the help of anyone who invoked his name. Amitabha is often portrayed flanked by the two popular Bodhisattvas, Avalokiteshvara and Mahasthamaprapta. Avolokiteshvara is the most compassionate of all Bodhisattvas – his 1,000 arms represent his tireless quest to bear his devotees to liberation.

The head of a Bodhisattva, from 8th-century Uttar Pradesh.

devotees as well as in their placing of the Buddha's function as a saviour above that of his personal triumph of detachment and enlightenment.

Whereas the Theravadins sought to imitate Gautama's world-denying path to liberation as conquerors (*arhants*) of ignorance, Mahayanists had as their goal the compassionate role of the Buddha as teacher and liberator. Mahayanist philosophers claimed that the Theravada path was selfish and limited, and they endorsed their argument by citing the example of Gautama's rejection of personal enlightenment when it was offered to him by the demon Mara (see p.33).

The Mahayana ideal was the Bodhisattva, the "Buddha-to-be" who sacrificed his own enlightenment in order to bring salvation to others. Portrayed as brilliant deities in Buddhist art, the Bodhisattvas were believed to have accumulated *karmic* merit from previous good deeds. Their ultimate act of self-sacrifice was in the distribution of this merit to their devotees. Praying in absolute faith to a Bodhisattva was said to lead automatically to rebirth in paradise.

According to the Mahayana version of the Sarnath sermon at the Deer Park (see p.34), the Buddha speaks directly to Maitreya, the future Buddha who is waiting in the heavens to be born some 5,000 years after his predecessor's death. The Buddha tells Maitreya that "having heard this Law and welcomed it with joy, go on now forever in happiness...[and]...where this pure doctrine prevails, even the householder becomes a Buddha".

The Mahayana Buddhists equated the personal experience of *nirvana* (enlightenment) with the absolute void (*sunyata*) that permeates the universe. The adepts who experience the reality of *nirvana* have the potential to become Buddhas themselves, provided that they follow the paths of compassion and contemplation that are central to Mahayanist thought.

Maitreya, the future Buddha, is depicted as a princely figure in this 4th-century sculpture from Gandhara, Pakistan.

Jainism

The word "Jain" is derived from the Sanskrit *jina*, meaning "conqueror", an epithet given to the twenty-four *Tirthankaras* or "Fordmakers" (see pp.42–3), who, through austerity, conquered their minds, passions and bodies to attain deliverance from the endless cycle of rebirth. Jainism is still the most ascetically demanding of all India's religions. Its purpose is not the glorification of an absolute god, but the attainment of self-perfection by the gradual

Mount Sarunjaya near Palitana in Gujarat, "the hill which conquers enemies", is one of the five holy mountains of Shvetambara Jainism.

abandonment of the material world. At the heart of Jain religion is the belief in an extreme form of *ahimsa* (non-violence), which demands that no living being should be hurt since, in the words of a Jain motto, "all living creatures must help each other".

Mahavira, last of the twenty-four Fordmakers, was the greatest of all Jain ascetics. From the moment of his renunciation, he went naked and is held to have had no concern for sleep, cleanliness, food or water. By imitating his life and through the eradication of all ties with the material world, Jain monks and nuns hope to follow him to liberation. Jain scriptures list ten reasons for renunciation – ranging from anger to the memory of previous births – which lead men and women to enter initiation (*diksha*) into asceticism.

The best-known part of the initiation is the ceremony in which the entrant pulls out his or her own hair in order to symbolize austerity and the abjuring of sexuality. Although Jain scriptures describe ceremonies in which naked

The Digambaras, or "sky-clad" monks, are one of the two principal Jain sects. Digambara ascetics reject possessions and wear no clothes.

SKY-CLAD MONKS

The 1st century BC saw a schism between the Digambara ("sky-clad") and Shvetambara ("white-clad") sects of Jainism. The Digambaras believe that ascetics should be "sky-clad" (naked) to imitate Mahavira's life of total abandonment, and to live in perfect accordance with the principle of non-violence. The Digambaras argue that clothes encourage a desire for possessions and increase the chance of life-forms being crushed. Unlike the Digambaras, the Shvetambaras wear some clothes and accept the possibility of deliverance for women Jains, who often outnumber Jain men almost two to one.

JAIN TEMPLES

Western India is renowned for its many temples that have been dedicated to different Fordmakers by wealthy Jain merchants. Jain communities continued to support temple building even after many parts of the country came under the sway of the Mughals in the 16th and 17th centuries. Jain temples are among the wealthiest in all India.

Ranakpur is the finest 16th-century Jain temple in Rajasthan. White marble is the principal material that was used in its construction, as can be seen in the finely worked columns (left) – of which there are 1,444 in total – and in the corbelled dome (above) that rises over the central hall in front of the main shrine.

monks pulled their hair out in great handfuls, many initiates today shave their heads before the ritual, leaving small tufts that are easier to extract. After ritually joining a Jain order, the ascetic takes five "great vows" (*mahavratas*) and promises to put them to good use. The first is the vow of total non-violence. The ascetic swears never to kill any life-form and to reject and repent of any acts of violence.

Jain non-violence governs every aspect of daily life. The ascetic should be careful when walking in case a life-form is harmed under his or her feet. Any speech that incites or suggests vio-lence must be avoided, as must any violent tendencies in the ascetic's own thoughts. All food and drink must be inspected in case a life-form is ingested, and care must be taken, when putting down an alms bowl, not to harm any creature. The ascetic is handed a brush to sweep insects from his or her path, and a mask is always worn to prevent breathing in tiny organisms. Jain ascetics may not prepare food, and they may only drink water that has first been strained.

The Fordmakers

The Jains recognize twenty-four *Tirthankaras*, or "Fordmakers", as their historical teachers. These figures are believed to have attained perfect wisdom (*kevala*), by breaking all bonds with the material world. Each *Tirthankara* belonged to the *kshatriyas* – kings and warriors from whose ranks the Buddha also came. With the exceptions of Parshva and Mahavira – the twenty-third and twenty-fourth *Tirthankaras* – they are legendary figures, inhabiting past "world ages" many millennia ago.

Each *Tirthankara* appeared at a time pre-ordained by the "turning of the wheel" (*avasarpini*) of the world ages. As the wheel descends, so do the physical stature and the lifespan of *Tirthankaras*, while the period of their

Gommateshvara, son of the first Fordmaker, Rishabha, is depicted in this colossal statue in Shravana Belgola, southern India. During the Mastakabhisheka festival the statue is bathed in milk, saffron and ghee, seen here as a spectacular shower of golden rain (above). The scale of the statue, which, at a height of 57 feet (18m), is one of the largest free-standing monuments in the world, can be gauged by the devotee placing offerings at his feet (below).

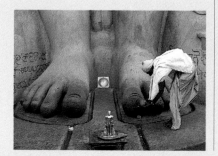

time on earth lessens. The earliest Ford-makers were fabled giants who had immeasurably long lives. The first, Rishabha, is said to have lived for millions of years; Mahavira, by contrast, had only a normal human lifespan.

The last Fordmaker, Mahavira, is credited with the founding of modern Jainism. He was a contemporary and rival of the Buddha (see pp.30–31), with whom his story has much in common. Both were of noble birth and renounced society at a similar time of life to wander with bands of ascetics. Like the teachings of the the Buddha, Mahavira's doctrine was based upon the possibility of release from desire, suffering and death, but whereas the Buddha taught the Middle Way between luxury and asceticism (see pp.34–5), Mahavira is famed for his severe asceticism and complete rejection of the material world. He is known as the greatest ascetic, the "most victorious conqueror" of mind and body.

The statue of Gommateshvara was erected in the 10th century and is a central place of worship for the Digambara sect of Jains.

PARSHVA

The twenty-third *Tirthankara* is said to have lived approximately 250 years before the birth of Mahavira. Parshva is best known for the story of his attainment of omniscience. He stood "sky-clad" (naked) in the yogic posture of "dismissing the body", having torn out all his hair. At that moment, the demon Meghamalin attacked him with apparitions, wild animals, darkness, great winds and rains, but Parshva was unmoved. As the demon king himself bore down upon the ascetic, the serpent king Dharanendra and his consort Lakshmi emerged from the earth to shelter him, and the terrified demon fled.

Parshva sits beneath the serpent king in this 15th-century palm-leaf manuscript from Gujurat.

Jain karma

These gilded sculptures in the Kanch Mandir temple at Indore in Madhya Pradesh show Jain Fordmakers who attained release from the material world by "burning off" the weight of their past karmas.

dust and so liberate it. For Jains, soul (*jiva*) is a living substance embodied in all life-forms: human beings, animals and even plants. Originally pure and all-knowing, *jiva* becomes tainted as it is shackled to a succession of bodies, accumulating *karmas*. Non-soul (*ajiva*) designates inanimate substance, whether material or not. The latter includes time and space, within which the soul struggles for release from matter.

The individual's ultimate goal, achievable only through many rebirths, is self-realization and the liberation of the soul. Because Jain *karma* is a

The most striking aspect of Jain *karma* is that it is perceived as a material entity, like a subtle dust that clogs the soul, binding it to the body. Many lifetimes are required to rid the soul of *karmic* result of negative actions, especially violence, whether of thought, word or deed, it is possible to avoid new *karma* particles by refraining from such actions. *Karma* already acquired in past

THE EIGHT KARMAS

The are eight forms of *karma*, half of which are harmful. Delusory *karma* (*mohaniya*) brings attachment to false ideas. Mental and spiritual confusion is caused by the *karma* that covers knowledge (*inanvaraniya*). A third (*darshanavaraniya*) obscures perception and

faith while a fourth (*antaraya*) *karma* is an obstacle to the energy of the soul.

The other four *karmas* are feeling (*vedaniya*) that governs the happiness of the soul; name (*nama*) *karma* that decides future rebirths, life (*ayus*) *karma* that decides the individual's lifespan, and clan (*gotra*) *karma* that determines social status.

lives must be eliminated by the process of *nijara*, undergoing austerities such as fasting and self-mortification, and the strict observance of the Three Jewels: right action, right faith and right knowledge.

Although early Jain texts insist that any act of violence, even if it is involuntary, attracts *karmic* dust, modern Jainism only considers an act to be *karmically* negative if it is "performed without care" (*pramada*).

The life of a Jain layperson is seen as a preparation for a future monastic life with its ascetic rigours, perhaps culminating in the final demonstration of non-attachment – *sallekhana* or ritual starvation, thought to enhance the soul's state in its next life. The soul is continually reborn until no new *karma* is acquired and any existing *karmic* stain has been wiped clean. Then the Jain attains the ultimate goal: release (*moksha*) or liberation of the pure soul.

THE HIGHEST VIRTUE

As all life-forms house a trapped *jiva* (soul), all are worthy of respect and compassion. The highest virtue in Jainism is total non-violence (*ahimsa*), the avoidance of any act that harms or kills another living being.

As they have the same number of senses, animals are credited with a *jiva*, and with near-human characteristics and the ability to control their behaviour and remember their past lives. As well as maintaining a strictly vegetarian diet, Jains build special rest homes where old or sick animals are cared for until they die from natural causes.

Jiva also resides in the vegetable kingdom, and plants are thought to share important characteristics of human life in their growth and decay, in their sensitivity to their surroundings, and in their consciousness. Jains generally refrain from consuming fruits with many seeds, and food or drink that undergoes change, such as the fermentation of alcohol.

Non-violence guides the choice of career for the layperson, and for this reason many Jains have been drawn to and excelled in commerce and finance. Their asceticism means that they save much of what they earn.

Mahatma Gandhi (see pp.150–51), himself from Gujurat, the centre of the Jain community from the 3rd century AD, was greatly influenced by the Jain doctrine of non-violence. He eventually used it as a highly effective political tactic, adopting the Jain motto "Non-violence is the highest religious duty" (*ahimsa paramo dharma*) in his civil-rights campaign.

This Shevtambara ascetic is shown carrying a mask to prevent himself from breathing in, and so killing, minute organisms. He also has a whisk with which to clear his path of small insects which he might squash.

The Forms of Vishnu

Above all else, early Hinduism is famed for its two great epics, the *Ramayana* and the *Mahabharata*, extraordinary narratives that celebrate the two most famous incarnations (*avatars*) of the god Vishnu. From *c.*500BC, a number of popular epics – whose tales of honour, love and war recounted the exploits of a new race of gods – superseded the *Vedas*, as a dynamic Hinduism began to evolve, characterized by exuberant devotionalism and a doctrine of disinterested action.

From these epics, particularly the *Puranas*, emerged the *trimurti*, the Hindu trinity: Brahma, the Creator; Vishnu, the Preserver; and Shiva, both Creator and Destroyer. The popularity of Vishnu and Shiva greatly exceeds that of Brahma, and it is in the *Ramayana* and the *Mahabharata* that the cult of Vishnu is most fully celebrated. The *Ramayana*, enacted in India to this day, tells the story of Rama, the seventh *avatar* of Vishnu, a hero whose honour and sense of duty surpass even his love for Sita, the tragic heroine. The *Mahabharata*, the story of a war between two dynasties, is probably the longest poem ever composed. Among the passages it contains is the *Bhagavad Gita*. At the heart of the action is the eighth *avatar* of Vishnu, Krishna, a mischievous lover and shrewd tactician, the best loved of all the Hindu gods.

Krishna, the eighth avatar *of Vishnu, is the most enduring symbol of the devotionalism that marked the classical period of Indian history. This 19th-century miniature from a* Bhagavata Purana *series depicts him as a pastoral god, protecting his herd from the evil intentions of Aghasura, a demon.*

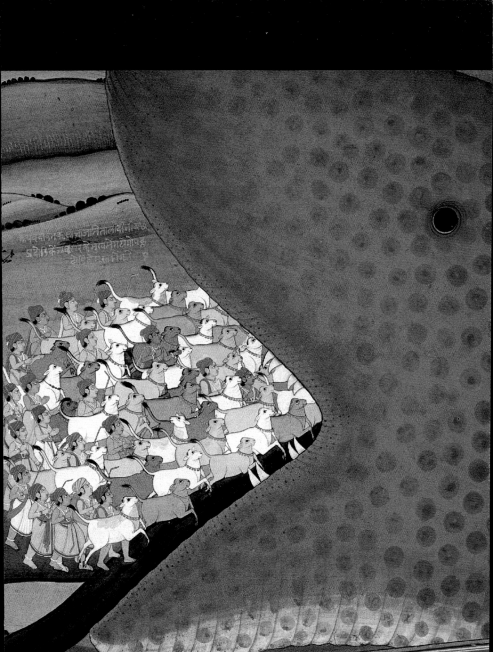

The trimurti

The bewildering array of deities and demons – traditionally 330 million – in the modern Hindu pantheon has its roots both in the Vedic gods and in the intellectual speculation of the *Upanishads* and "forest philosophies". But from the 4th to the 12th centuries AD, the growth of a more popular religion, based around the *Puranas*, placed at its heart the *trimurti* of Brahma, Vishnu and Shiva.

Brahma is the personified creator of the universe. He is the most abstract of the three deities, and is often considered a fusion of Prajapati, the creator god of the *Vedas*, and the utterly impersonal concept of *brahman* (godhead). Brahma is also he who "brings diversity into unity", a mediator between Vishnu and Shiva, who represent opposites.

Vishnu (the Preserver) is the protector of *dharma* (righteousness) and the guardian of humanity. He is a solar deity who fights on the side of good and comes down to earth to help humankind. His most famous incarnations, or *avatars*, are Krishna and Rama, the heroes of the epics the *Mahabharata* (see pp.56–7) and the *Ramayana* (see pp.52–3).

The last of the *trimurti* is Shiva (the Auspicious One), simultaneously destroyer

and creator. Shiva is the Lord of Yoga, worshipped as the *linga* (see pp.66–7), whose dance, to the beat of his own drum, is said to be the rhythm of the universe. He is the most ambivalent of the three gods of the *trimurti* because of his destructive aspect.

Just as the *atman* (soul) was thought to mirror *brahman*, so the fast-evolving Hindu pantheon was seen to embody the many forms that *brahman* must assume to make itself knowable in the material world. The Hindu gods thus represent the visible and manifest aspects of godhead. Unlike *brahman*, they act within this world, answering prayers, fighting evil or destroying illusion (*maya*). Each Hindu god is simply an aspect of *brahman*, and a devotee may choose any one of them as the main object of his or her veneration.

A devotee's *ishta* (personal deity) is worshipped as a representative of the total godhead, and although every god and goddess bears particular attributes and powers, they are not completely distinct but share many of the same characteristics. To a Hindu, there is nothing heretical or paradoxical in proclaiming any one of a number of deities as the Lord of the Universe.

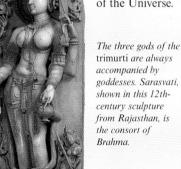

Vishnu appears in many forms, the most popular being the ten avatars. The first avatar is the fish, or Matsya, represented in this modern plaster statue from Tamil Nadu.

The three gods of the trimurti are always accompanied by goddesses. Sarasvati, shown in this 12th-century sculpture from Rajasthan, is the consort of Brahma.

BRAHMA

Brahma, the creator, is a
significant Hindu god,
despite the fact that he has
few devotees or temples
dedicated to his worship.
Even in medieval India it
seems likely that his
popularity was limited. He
is said to have created the
universe and then withdrawn,
leaving its maintenance to
Vishnu, the Preserver. This
perhaps explains his lack of
appeal. Brahma is often
depicted with four faces
turned towards the four
points of the compass, his
four hands holding the four
books of the *Vedas*. His
heads are usually crowned
and his faces bearded, giving
him the appearance of a wise,
compassionate old man. He
is sometimes depicted on a
lotus that emerges from
Vishnu's navel, a reference to
his being "born of a lotus".

*Brahma is depicted in this
12th-century temple at
Halebid in Karnataka, with
three of his four heads visible.*

THE PURANAS

The *Puranas*, or Antiquities,
rank with the *Vedas* as sacred
Hindu texts. They were compiled between the 4th and
12th centuries AD, but their
origins are far older.
Attributed to the sage Vyasa,
the supposed author of the
Mahabharata (see pp.56–7),
the *Puranas* contain a massive bulk of mythological
material from which much of
the dazzling pantheons and
epics of later Hinduism were
drawn. They list entire dynasties, descended both from

Manu, mythical ancestor of
the human race, and from the
deities and heroes of the
Mahabharata, while their
prophecies predict future
royal dynasties.

The *Puranas* are written
in simple language and are
seldom highly mystical or
hard to understand or
interpret. They list sacred
sites and pilgrimages, specify
caste relations and give
instructions for the portrayal
of divine images.

Much of their importance
lies in the fact that the
language in which they are

written is accessible to
women and to those of low
caste who were prevented
from reading the more
esoteric *Veda* texts, which
were reserved for men of the
brahmin caste.

The eighteen principal
Puranas are dedicated to the
trimurti. They provide not
only the mythological
background from which
many of the tales of the gods
were fashioned, but also the
origins of more abstract
theological concepts such
as *dharma*, *karma* and the
nature of *atman*.

Avatars of Vishnu

In the books of the *Vedas*, Vishnu appears only rarely, as the junior partner of the great god Indra. His most famous exploit, recounted in the Vedic hymns, was his "measuring" of the universe with three giant strides to claim it for humanity from the demon kings. The myth tells of his might and omnipresence which were developed by later authors into a power greater than Indra's, such that the Vedic king of the gods was eventually forced to ask Vishnu for help.

In the *Puranas*, Vishnu is depicted as Lord of the Universe and Protector of Humanity. His attributes are the disk (*chakra*), the conch shell (*shankha*), the club (*gada*), and the lotus (*padma*). His consort is Lakshmi, the beautiful goddess of wealth, honour, faith and love, who sits on a lotus flower.

Vishnu is best known, however, through his *avatars*, the incarnations that he assumes to assist humanity in its struggle against darkness. Early on, he was credited with as many as twenty-eight *avatars*, as the deities of the Vedic pantheon were incorporated into the later epics, but by the 8th century AD he was widely recognized as having ten. The first three *avatars* (Matsya, a fish, Kurma, a tortoise, and Varaha, a boar) are mythological creatures, drawn from cosmogonic accounts in the *Vedas*, none of whom were linked with Vishnu in the original texts. The fourth *avatar*, Narasimha, is a man-lion who rescues the world from a terrible demon, while the fifth, Vamana, is a dwarf who claims the universe for humanity by covering it with three strides. This tale has clear links with the Vedic exploits that were attributed to Vishnu.

The sixth *avatar* is Parashurama, "Rama with the axe", who killed many arrogant barons and warriors. His inclusion in the pantheon may reflect strife between the *brahmins* and the *kshatriyas*, as each class vied for power and influence. Rama and Krishna, the seventh and eighth *avatars* of Vishnu, are the resplendent heroes of the *Ramayana* (see pp.52–3) and the *Mahabharata* (see pp.56–7), and it is above all from them that Vishnu derives his reputation as lord and benign protector of humanity. The ninth *avatar* is the Buddha, despite the hostility of many Buddhist teachings to Hindu beliefs. The Buddha's inclusion is a remarkable testament to Hinduism's ability to evolve by absorbing and redefining any culture or doctrine that rose to challenge it. Finally there is Kalki, the future *avatar*, who will appear at the end of this world age to punish the wicked, reward the pious and return the universe to *brahman*.

GARUDA

Vishnu's mount is the eagle Garuda. Like Nandi, Shiva's bull, Garuda is invoked as a god himself, eager to help humanity against demons. Garuda's great gift to humankind was *soma*, the nectar of immortality that he stole from the gods.

This 18th-century illustration shows Garuda flying to the aid of humans with armed avatars of Vishnu on his back.

The panelled doors to the Swaminarayana temple at Bhuj in Gujarat are painted with Vishnu's ten avatars; above them is Krishna, with a lotus below his feet, flanked by cows, a monkey and an angel.

The Ramayana

The *Ramayana,* one of the great Sanskrit epic poems, helped to develop a more popular, devotional religion. A product of the less exclusive world of the *kshatriya* ethic, it is not so heavily dominated by the *brahmin*-controlled sacrificial and ritual elements of Hinduism. It remains a popular source of religious teaching, through public readings and dramatizations.

The core of the epic poem was first composed in the 4th century BC as a secular tale recited by bards who were attendant on the royal courts. However, as the centuries passed, the religious elements of the story were expanded upon, and Rama, its hero, became transformed

Crowds gather in Ramnagar near Varanasi, during the ten-day performance of the Ramalila.

from a warrior king into a warrior deity. By the 4th century AD, Rama was widely identified as the seventh incarnation of the Hindu god, Vishnu.

The *Ramayana's* links with Vedic religion are, however, still strong. *Brahmin* priests are widely honoured in its verses, and the horse sacrifice (see p.17) plays a crucial part in the narrative. Like the *Vedas* (see pp.16–17) and the *Mahabharata* (see pp.56–7), the *Ramayana* is believed to have been divinely revealed: the story is supposed to have come to its composer, Valmiki, while he was meditating upon the *mantra* "Ram". Valmiki's own life assumes mythic proportions in the introduction to the main text, in which he plays an active role. Legend has it that he retired to the forest where, during 1,000 years of meditation, he kept so motionless that his body became covered by a *valmika* (anthill) – hence his name, meaning "son of the anthill".

Despite the secular nature of the poem in its original form, the narrative scheme of the *Ramayana* clearly shows the influence of essentially Vedic elements. In its early pages, for example, Rama is frequently linked with the glorious Vedic sun god Indra and with the battle against evil. Like Indra, Rama is an ideal warrior, and – unlike the confused Arjuna of the *Mahabharata* – he never hesitates to raise his bow, and clearly draws the battle lines between good and evil.

THE RAMALILA

The festival of Dasahra celebrates Rama's victory over Ravana and his demon army. During nine days of fasting, the epic tale of Rama and Sita is narrated throughout India, and in the *Ramalila* it is acted out with music, dance and elaborate costumes. Celebrations climax with Sita's rescue, and huge effigies of Ravana, his brother Kumbhakarna and son Maghanada, are paraded through the streets – stuffed with fireworks, they explode in colour when set alight by an effigy of Rama.

A painted paper effigy, from Delhi, of the demon king Ravana, Rama's great enemy.

RAMA AND SITA

Rama's actions in the *Ramayana* epic are governed by *dharma*, the irrefutable law that is the foundation of both the cosmic and the social orders. Although the *Ramayana* is a tale of martial glory, it is also a corpus of moral and ethical precepts, providing a guide to statesmanship, human conduct and relationships.

Rama is an idealized figure, a perfect king, warrior and husband. The epic traces his life, beginning with his birth as the eldest son of the good king Dasharatha. He wins Sita – the epitome of purity – for his wife. But on the eve of their accession, they are denied the throne, and sent into exile for fourteen years by Rama's father. Typically, Rama acts with honour: in accordance with the rule of *dharma*, he obeys his father, who then dies of sorrow. Rama does not return until he has served the full term of his exile. He roams the wilderness with Sita, fulfilling his caste duty by protecting *brahmin* hermits from local demons. The greatest demon, Ravana, kidnaps Sita and takes her to Lanka (Sri Lanka). Rama's devotion leads him to spend many years in search of her.

The narrative climaxes with Sita's eventual rescue, as Rama and his monkey ally Hanuman (see pp.54–5) obliterate the capital of the demon kingdom. The lovers are finally reunited but still Rama puts *dharma* above his own interests, and in a tragic denouement he banishes Sita. Although he knows her to be pure, the *dharma* of a king decrees that her time spent in the company of another man brings him dishonour. Still loyal to her husband, Sita prays to the earth to swallow her up, and Rama is left to mourn her loss until he too offers himself to the god of death.

Scenes from the Ramayana *are a favourite topic in Indian miniature painting: Rama and Sita seated in exile, with Hanuman kneeling at their feet (above); an energetic depiction of the siege of Lanka (left), from an early 17th-century Mughal painting on paper, now in the National Museum of New Delhi.*

Hanuman

Hanuman, the *Ramayana's* monkey hero, is Rama's most loyal devotee. He is the embodiment of *bhakti* (devotion), who gladly offers his own life in the service of his god. He is the son of Vayu, Vedic god of the wind, from whom he inherited the strength of hurricanes and the power to fly. The swiftest of the epic warrior-heroes, Hanuman also possesses the ability to metamorphose into whatever form he chooses.

The *Ramayana* relates that after his divine birth, Hanuman grew stronger and wiser with every passing year, destroying local demons, slaying rogue elephants, and even flying up to grasp the rising sun, which he mistook for an apple. One day while Hanuman and his master, the exiled monkey king, Sugriva, were hiding in a forest, they met Rama and his brother Lakshmana. Rama related the story of the kidnapping of his wife, Sita, by the demon Ravana, and his search for the place where the demon king had taken her. Deeply moved, Hanuman realized that his destiny was to serve at Rama's side, and he rallied an army for that purpose.

When the monkey army failed to find Ravana and his hostage, it was Hanuman who discovered the demon's hideout in Lanka. He assumed the form of an ordinary monkey to escape legions of powerful demons, so that he could enter Ravana's magnificent palace.

Hanuman found Sita sitting dejectedly in a garden, surrounded by demonesses. He emerged from his hiding place to

A masked player enacts the exploits of Hanuman in a performance of stories from the Ramayana.

comfort her. Seeing a talking monkey, she swooned, but was reassured by the ring that Hanuman had brought from Rama. He told his story and swore that Rama was destitute without her. The monkey offered Sita the chance to escape by flying on his back, but Sita refused out of respect for her husband, whose honour would be tainted if she were rescued by anyone but him.

To prepare the way for the battle that lay ahead, Hanuman taunted the demon king, smashing the city walls and annihilating thousands of demon guards. In revenge, the king set fire to Hanuman's tail. Growing to an enormous size, the monkey ran through the city with his burning tail, setting buildings ablaze, before returning to Rama with the message from his wife, Sita. Hanuman and the monkey armies destroyed Lanka and its demon king, and Sita was reunited with her lord.

When the guru Ramananda brought devotionalism (*bhakti*) from southern India to the north in the 14th century AD, Hanuman became one of its principal deities. Ramananda's followers worship Rama as the supreme deity, and honour Hanuman as Rama's greatest devotee. Due to his shape-shifting skills, Hanuman is also revered by the *bhakti* movement as a powerful magician and *siddha* (possessor of occult powers).

This 18th-century engraving depicts the battle between Rama and the multi-headed demon Ravana, and shows Hanuman poised for action.

HANUMAN'S HEART

In the concluding chapter of the *Ramayana*, Hanuman's devotion to Rama is further elaborated. The monkey armies finally finished their celebrations after the triumphal victory over Lanka and prepared to return home from Rama's palace. Only Hanuman was left, but he declared that he must stay to serve Rama and his queen, Sita. Sugriva, the monkey king, asked for proof of

Hanuman's devotion, at which the most loyal of all devotees tore open his own chest to reveal images of Rama and Sita within.

A modern plaster statue of Hanuman shows him tearing open his chest to reveal Rama and Sita inside it.

The Mahabharata

This modern painting depicts the Contest of the Princes, *an episode in the* Mahabharata.

The *Mahabharata* ("Great Epic of the Bharata Dynasty") was originally entitled *Jaya* ("Victory"). With over 100,000 stanzas it is perhaps the longest poem ever composed. It stands, with the *Ramayana* (see pp.52–3), as one of the two great Sanskrit epics. It was probably begun in the 4th or 3rd centuries BC, but many amendments were made and it was not completed until the end of the Gupta dynasty in the 4th century AD. Much of the material is far older, however, dating back to the Vedic period; some of the stories would have been familiar to audiences as early as 1000BC. Indra, the Vedic sun god, is mentioned several times in earlier parts of the text, for example, although by the 4th century BC he was scarcely more than a figure from folklore.

Krishna (see pp.62–3) appears in the epic, as the leader of his people and an ally of the Pandavas. He still appears more a superhuman warrior than a god in his battles alongside the Pandavas, but he grows in stature to emerge finally as the divine teacher of humanity.

According to legend, the entire *Mahabharata* was dictated by Vyasa to the elephant-headed god Ganesha (see pp.72–3), who made one condition: he would only agree to write it down if it were told without a pause. However fast it was dictated, Ganesha kept pace. At one time he broke off a tusk to use in place of a damaged stylus so as not to interrupt the flow of sacred words. The denser, more speculative passages were apparently attempts to slow the deity down, forcing him to stop and think whenever the meaning became unclear.

The central plot of the *Mahabharata* concerns two dynasties, the Pandavas and Kauravas. The rival families are cousins, the sons of Vyasa's two sons: the blind Dhritarashtra and the pious Pandu. Dhritarashtra is the eldest, but, because he is blind, Pandu is made king. Pandu has five sons: the eldest and righteous Yudhishthira; Bhima of ferocious strength; Arjuna the skilled warrior; and the twins Nakula and Sahadeva. Dhritarashtra, on the other hand, has 100 sons, the eldest of whom is the scheming Duryodhana.

When Pandu dies, his blind but well-intentioned brother, Dhritarashtra, takes Pandava's sons into his own palace. In time Dhritarashtra divides the kingdom, giving half of it to

Yudhishthira and half to Duryodhana. However, Duryodhana becomes jealous of the affection his father feels for his cousin, and even more so of the lands that the Pandavas have inherited. Through trickery and cunning, the Pandavas are forced into exile, and have to wait thirteen years before they have a chance to reclaim their kingdom. This is the cause of the terrible war that follows, resulting in the destruction of the entire race except for one survivor, who continues the dynasty. This war forms the backdrop to the *Bhagavad Gita*.

VYASA

The legendary author of the *Mahabharata*, the sage Vyasa (whose name in Sanskrit means "Compiler"), boasted that "that which cannot be found here exists nowhere". Vyasa was reputedly the son of the ascetic Parasara and the Dasa princess Satyavati. Called "the Homer of the East" (although far more has been ascribed to him than to the Greek poet), Vyasa is said to have composed the entire *Mahabharata* and all eighteen *Puranas* (see p.49), besides compiling the four books of the *Vedas* (see pp.16–17). He was also a priest and teacher.

Many writers now consider Vyasa to be a composite name for the many *brahmins* who worked on the text over the centuries, but he also has a vital place in the narrative. He is the father of some of the principal characters in the epic – the opposed dynasties of the Sons of Darkness and the Sons of Light – and he himself often appears in the story to advise characters in need or to soothe the distressed.

This 18th-century manuscript depicts Vyasa as a seated bearded sage, dictating the Mahabharata *to the elephant-headed Ganesha, with Durga above and Brahma below.*

Bhakti

Krishna's love for Radha symbolizes bhakti *devotion in this 19th-century painting,*

Bhakti (in later Sanskrit, "reverent devotion") was a movement which stressed the emotional attachment and love of a devotee for his or her personal god. It therefore implied a dualistic relationship between worshipper and god. Although all major deities in the Hindu pantheon had devotional cults, *bhakti* has been especially common in the worship of Krishna, an *avatar* of Vishnu. In the *Bhagavad Gita*, (see pp.60–61), Krishna taught *bhakti yoga* ("the way of devotion"), placing it above other paths to salvation through *karma* (ritual activity) and *jnana* (spiritual knowledge). He declared to his devotees: "Worshipping me with love, I bestow the rule of understanding, whereby they come to me".

The *bhakti* movement reached its height from *c*.AD500 to *c*.AD1500, starting in southern India before spreading north. Its chief characteristic was an intensely emotional worship, expressed in terms of personal love, yearning, courtship and ecstasy. *Bhakti* cults reacted against the rigid exclusivity of the *brahmin* priests, with their elaborate rituals that required a knowledge of Sanskrit. They often rejected the role of the priest as an intermediary between devotee and deity, teaching instead that divine grace was available to all, irrespective of caste or sex. While *bhakti* scholars filled the temples of southern India, bands of devotees travelled the countryside, visiting shrines, singing devotional hymns and engaging local holy men in debate.

All *bhakti* sects shared the basic doctrine of divine grace and ecstatic love. *Bhakti* poets wrote of an intensity of guilt and a yearning for redemption familiar to Christian theology. Like the New Testament, the *bhakti* sects taught that divine love could also be expressed through love of one's neighbours, whatever their social status. But unlike Christian churches, *bhakti* sects welcomed women into their priesthood.

Bhakti adherents were opponents of Buddhism and Jainism, and they had hastened the decline of both in southern India by the 10th century. The arrival of the Muslims in the Ganges basin from the 12th century onward paradoxically also helped the *bhakti* movement, for *brahmins* with their ritualized Hinduism found it harder to survive without royal support than *bhakti* devotees. *Bhakti* devotionalism even affected Islam: there are Muslim poems which start with the standard invocation of Allah, but go on to claim that Krishna is one of the Muslim prophets.

THE LINGAYATS

The Lingayat sect was founded in the 12th century by Basava, a Shaivite *brahmin* who at the age of sixteen threw away the sacred thread marking his priestly caste to propagate a message of social equality, rejecting orthodox Hinduism. Seeing no need for a priest to mediate between Shiva and his devotees, Basava instructed his

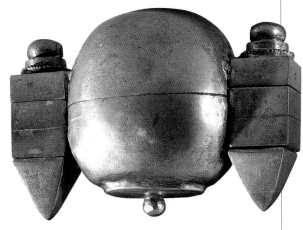

Reading sacred texts is a popular act of bhakti.

Devotees of Shiva belonging to the Lingayat sect wear silver containers holding miniature lingas *around their necks.*

followers to wear a small *linga* (see pp.66–7) about their necks and worship Shiva directly. This explains their name, the Lingayats. Basava rejected the authority of the *Vedas* and the *brahmin* caste, declaring that sacred texts were useless if they did not lead to a personal experience of God. Basava married two untouchable women, and encouraged equal rights for women and the demolition of all caste barriers. When marriage between a *brahmin's* daughter and an untouchable led a local king to persecute Basava's followers, they rose in rebellion and Basava himself was killed.

THE ALVARS

Twelve Alvars (Vaishnavite saints) are recognized as founders of Vaishnavite *bhakti* in southern India. Their hymns to Vishnu and his *avatars* were intensely emotional. Of over 4,000 hymns, most were composed by the Alvars Tirumangai and Nammalvar. One Alvar king, Kulashekhara, so loved Rama that he raised an army to rescue Sita, the deity's consort, from demons.

Praying to temple deities is the usual form of bhakti. *This worshipper has offered his hair as a token of devotion at Tirupati in Andhra Pradesh.*

MADHVA

The 13th-century philosopher Madhva was one of the most striking and extreme dualist teachers. His prodigious output included commentaries on the *Brahmasutra* and *Bhagavad Gita*, as well as thirty-five other works. Most unusually for a Hindu, he rejected the theory of *maya* (see pp.130–31) saying the material world, although transitory, was real. Madhva also believed in eternal damnation and salvation. He was perhaps influenced by Nestorian Christians, for his life has many parallels with that of Christ, most notably his miracles.

The Bhagavad Gita

A modern printed version of the Bhagavad Gita, *showing the warrior Arjuna to whom Krishna delivered his great sermon.*

The *Bhagavad Gita* ("Song of the Lord") is one of the most important and popular of Indian religious texts, although it is not strictly speaking a *shruta* (a divinely revealed text such as the *Vedas*). It is a comparatively brief episode within the *Mahabharata* consisting of 700 verses in eighteen chapters written in a semi-dialogue form.

It opens with two vast armies facing each other on the "field of *dharma*". On each side are tens of thousands of fearsome warriors, as well as gods, demons and giants with supernatural weapons. These were the armies of the Pandavas and Kauravas, cousins and rivals for a single throne. The most glorious warrior of all was Arjuna, so skilled in the arts of battle that he was thought invincible. His charioteer was Krishna, Lord of the Universe (see pp.62–3), and behind Arjuna stood legions of mighty allies ready to do battle in his name.

At that moment, as the final trumpets sounded and the air filled with dread, Arjuna looked at the army opposing him and weakness overcame him. "Facing us in the field of battle are teachers, fathers and sons ... I do not wish to kill these people, even if I myself am killed. Not even for the kingdom of the three worlds: how much less for a kingdom of this earth!" said the warrior to Krishna. "What happiness could we have if we killed our own kinsmen? ... I will not fight," he said, and then fell silent. Krishna smiled and spoke the verses which form the *Bhagavad Gita*.

Krishna first appealed to Arjuna's honour and *dharmic* duty as a *kshatriya* (see p.25). "There is no greater good for a warrior than to fight in a righteous war," he said, adding that there was no need to be sorrowful about what was inevitable. "Arjuna, you grieve because you think that you are the doer of your actions," he continued. "Think instead of God as the doer. You are but an instrument in his hands. You are only

THE THREE PATHS

The discipline or path of action (*karma* yoga) which Krishna outlined to Arjuna as he hesitated before the battle is not the only way to *brahman* which the *Bhagavad Gita* acknowledged, although it has proved very popular with those who must live and struggle in the world. Mahatma Gandhi was only one of many people in the 20th century inspired by this passage. The other two paths are the discipline of knowledge (*jnana* yoga), in which release is sought through asceticism and contemplative retreat from the world in a way comparable to Buddhism, and devotion to God (*bhakti* yoga). This is considered the highest form of yoga, and in it the self humbly worships God, hoping less for a release from reincarnation than for an ecstatic divine vision. In return for such worship, God extends his favour to his devotees, thereby enables them to transcend their earthly bonds. All three of the paths share the belief that God is manifest in every single aspect of life, including nature and society.

carrying out his will."But Arjuna was still uncertain. "How can I kill my kinsmen?" he asked, and sank again into despondency, his great bow lying useless on his knees. Krishna answered in one of the best-known passages of the *Bhagavad Gita*. "Death is not final," he told Arjuna. "If any man thinks that he slays, and if another thinks that he is slain, neither knows the truth. The Eternal in man cannot kill: the Eternal in man cannot die. The soul in man is neither born nor does it die. Weapons cannot cut it; fire cannot burn it ... What makes you think that you can destroy the soul?"

Krishna, having defined the *atman* (see pp.24–5) in every person, revealed a new way of releasing the soul from the cycles of reincarnation: the discipline of action, *karma* yoga (see p.86). As opposed to the Buddhist and Jain paths of asceticism and renunciation, this is a

yoga of positive action, a way to *brahman* (godhead) that can be followed by anyone, however immersed in worldly affairs. Krishna argued that it is not acts in themselves which bind people to the round of rebirth, but the selfish intentions so often behind them. The true opposite of selfish action is disinterested or selfless action; total inaction is anyway impossible.

In the *Bhagavad Gita*, action is no longer the sole cause of *karma*. The yoga that Krishna taught Arjuna offers a path to enlightenment based on the abandonment of desire. An enlightened mind, he says, is indifferent "to pleasure and pain, gain and loss". "Prepare yourself for the fight," he tells Arjuna. "Whatever you do, do it as an offering to me." Arjuna therefore returned to the world of battle, and his path has since been followed by millions of Hindus.

Arjuna and Krishna on the battlefield, the latter turning his head to deliver the famous sermon known as the Bhagavad Gita, *from a 19th-century manuscript.*

Krishna

Krishna is both the most charming and the most accessible of the major Hindu deities. He is a loyal ally of humans, who stops at nothing to help his friends. He is also a crafty foe. Krishna is the eighth *avatar* of Vishnu, sent to earth to combat evil and fight for good, whenever *dharma* (righteousness) is threatened by the forces of darkness.

The first evidence of a Krishna cult in India appears in texts and artefacts from the 4th to the 2nd centuries BC. The Krishna of this time is Krishna Vasudeva, probably a historical figure who was born in Dwaraka. His heroic adventures earned him fame as a warrior and head of his native Yadava clan, whose territories increased with Krishna's growing reputation. The Yadava hero is thought to have become the leader of a religious cult, and was deified as Bhagavat, "the blessed one", from which the *Bhagavad Gita* (see pp.60–61) drew its name.

The legend of Krishna holding up Govardhan mountain to shield the herds from the storm of Indra is illustrated in this sculptured wall panel from the 12th-century temple at Halebid in southern India.

In the *Mahabharata*, particularly the *Bhagavad Gita*, Krishna often appears as the perfect ally, skilful in war and loyal to the end. He slays enemies with an appetite even greater than the

BALARAMA

In early Krishna worship, Krishna's entire family were objects of devotion. The second half of the *Harivamsa*, "Chronicle of Hari" (an alternative name for Krishna), recounts the exploits of his descendants. Krishna's sister and brother played major roles in later cults of Vishnu. Only his brother, Balarama, knew of Krishna's constantly mischievous intentions. Balarama was originally an agricultural deity, linked with ploughing and fertility, and is strongly associated with pre-Aryan *naga* (snake) worship (see pp.68–9).

KRISHNA CENTRES

The worship of Krishna is popular all over India with sacred shrines concentrated in the north of the country (see map below). Popular prints and posters showing Krishna (see inset below) are sold to visitors when they visit these shrines and then distributed among relatives and friends on the return home.

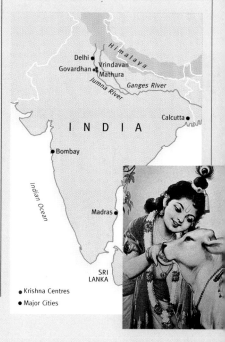

Pandava brothers', to whose aid he comes. But in some passages, Krishna is not all-virtuous. At times he is mischievous, unscrupulous and deceitful. Not only mortal enemies are defeated by Krishna: the Vedic deities Indra and Varuna bow before his might, and even Shiva, the fearsome destroyer, is defeated by him.

Krishna subduing the serpent-demon Kaliya, shown in a 10th-century bronze.

As Krishna's reputation grew in the early centuries AD, the deeds of other deities were attributed to him. When Krishna was born, he miraculously escaped his uncle who had ordered that every newborn child must die. When the infant Krishna was being rescued, the waters of the River Juma parted and he was carried in a basket to safety – a story which has clear parallels with the Bible stories of Moses and Jesus.

Krishna is the principle deity of the *bhakti* movement that flourished from *c.*AD 500 to *c.*AD1500 (see pp.58–9). He was worshipped as the embodiment of divine love and as the most mischievous expression of "divine play" (*lila*).

THE SEDUCTION OF THE GOPIS

Krishna's seduction of the *gopis*, the wives and daughters of the cowherds, is represented in song, painting and popular culture throughout India. On Sharad Purnima (the full moon in November), Krishna, the story goes, went to his favourite spot in the forest and began to play his flute. As the divinely sweet notes reached the village, the *gopis* were entranced and, mad with desire, they followed the music. A whirling frenzy of dancing and passion ensued and even the gods and the dead descended to earth to witness the spectacle. The *Brahmavaivarta Purana* describes a lush glade ripe with swelling fruit and loud with the buzz of honeybees. Among the 900,000 *gopis*, "like a jewel in the midst of her company", was Radha. Krishna, overcome by love, dropped his flute, and "even

the clothing dropped from his body". Although he ravished every one of the *gopis* in the thirty-three-day dance, he embraced Radha all the time. This story is astounding for the detailed extravagance of its eroticism.

Performances of the story of Krishna and Radha are usually enacted by boys. This production takes place at Brindavan in northern India, the setting of many of Krishna's exploits.

Krishna playing the flute to the gopis and the cowherds is a popular subject in Indian miniature painting.

Shiva and the Goddess

Whereas Vishnu is constant and easily definable in his fight for righteousness, Shiva is the most ambiguous of the world's major deities. He is phallic, always erect, yet never sheds his semen, the Lord of the Cremation ground yet a symbol of regeneration, the paragon of the silent power of ascetic concentration and also the wild wind of change.

As Lord of Yoga, Shiva transcends the illusory nature of reality. Whereas Vishnu incarnates himself to act in this world, Shiva remains aloof, and is portrayed either meditating in hidden reaches of the Himalayas or in his abstract form as the *linga*, symbolic of the phallus. Shiva's power (*shakti*) to act in reality is embodied instead in female forms, as his consorts Sati and Parvati, and as the destroyer goddesses Kali and Durga, all of whom are in turn aspects of Devi, the great Goddess. The very land of India is said to be the body of the Goddess and she is thus knowable and approachable to her devotees.

Parvati is the Daughter of the Himalayas, and the stories relating her mythological life with Shiva are rooted in the mountains. With their children, the elephant-headed Ganesha and the warrior god Skanda, they are the "divine family" of Hindu myth, and their mythological lives are symbolically re-enacted by *sadhus* (renunciants).

The head of Shiva within the yoni *(see p.66) of shakti, surrounded by a serpent and accompanied by the trident of the god, as imagined by the modern tribal artist, Janagadh Singh Shyam, who lives in Madhya Pradesh, central India.*

Shiva linga

A Shiva linga *set in a white-marked* yoni *beside the Ganges at Varanasi, the city sacred to Shiva.*

The *linga* (phallus) is worshipped as the incarnate form of Shiva and is a vivid representation of the god's dual nature. Although he is the god of ascetics, renunciation and yoga, Shiva is mainly worshipped as the phallus, a symbol of eroticism and sexual energy.

The Shiva *linga* is forever erect because it swells with potential creation – Shiva never sheds but always retains his semen. Even before the full emergence of the Tantric movement (see pp.110–11), which used sexual imagery to represent the union of opposites, the *linga* was depicted arising from the *yoni*, a symbol of the vulva or of female energy. The *linga* and the *yoni* denote the union of male and female, heaven and earth, and are a powerful representation of the totality of existence.

In the compendium of legends known as the *Linga Purana*, a guru explains the worship of the Shiva *linga* by recounting a well-known myth which occurred long ago when the universe was shrouded in darkness and the world was flooded by water. Vishnu and Brahma were arguing, each declaring himself to be the greatest of the

IMAGES OF SHIVA

The *ekamukha linga*, which has an image of Shiva carved upon one side, is a "bridge" between the abstract and iconic forms of the deity. Shiva is also sometimes represented with four or five heads, signifying his various aspects. One head may show him as Bhairava, his incarnation as a wild ascetic, others may portray him in his wrathful, meditative or hermaphrodite form.

An ekamukha Shiva linga *in red sandstone from a 5th-century temple in central India.*

A brass cover for a one-faced Shiva linga set in a yoni, made in a modern Vrindabar workshop.

gods, when suddenly a great pillar of fire appeared from the waters – it was so tall that it seemed to be unending.

The two gods set out to discover the height and depth of the pillar. Vishnu assumed the form of a boar and dived into the water, while Brahma turned himself into a swan and flew as high as he could. Both returned amazed that they had failed to find the pillar's extremities. Shiva then appeared and explained that the flaming pillar was the cosmic form of the *linga*, the earthly symbol of his incarnate power.

A quite different legend describing the origin of the Shiva *linga* tells of a group of sages who were practising asceticism in the forest without an adequate understanding of the greatness of Shiva. To punish them, Shiva appeared as a naked yogi, filthy from performing austerities, and seduced the sages' wives. Furious, the ascetics castrated him, but, at the moment that his *linga* fell to the ground, the universe was engulfed in darkness. The sages realized their error and begged Shiva to restore light to the world. He agreed on condition that, from that time onward, the sages should worship him in the form of the *linga*.

A self-manifested linga *(see below), made from a river-washed stone, decorated with sandalwood paste and a fresh hibiscus.*

LINGA WORSHIP

Lingas are usually carved from stone, but they can also be fashioned in sand or made from pebbles or an anthill. Particularly sacred are the *svayambhu* ("self-manifested") *lingas* that appear in natural formations, such as the Amarnath *linga* that is formed from ice. The *linga,* as with any icon, is often anointed with milk and ghee, and offerings of fruits, sweets, leaves and flowers are placed on it.

Snakes, cows and bulls

In Indian art and religion, cows, bulls and snakes (particularly the cobra) have a powerful symbolic value. They are specifically sacred to Shiva, but elements of snake (*naga*) and cow worship are evident in the attributes and myths of most of the major Hindu deities. Snakes and cows draw much of their symbolic power from their ambiguity: the snake is both a destroyer and a guardian of human life, while the cow's fertility and nurturing qualities are balanced by the bull's more aggressive instincts.

The worship of snake deities is thought to have preceded the Vedic religion of the Aryan warrior invaders (see pp. 12–13), and is still very common in rural southern India.

The importance of *naga* cults is evident from the prevalence of *naga* deities in the major Indian religions. The great serpent Shesha is the "endless one" in Hindu myth, whose form embodies the Milky Way, and whose four great coils stand for the four *yugas* (world ages) of cosmic time. Buddhist myth recounts the tale of Muchilinda, a snake-king

NANDI

The respect that is accorded the bull in modern-day India is a consequence of its association with Shiva. Shiva's mount is the great white bull Nandi whom the Hindu god

A statue of the sacred bull Nandi, decorated with a garland of flowers, from a Shiva temple in Varanasi.

rides into battle against the demons. In many Shaivite temples a statue of Nandi faces the entrance to the main shrine so that he may watch over his master – he is the most loyal of the deity's protectors. Paintings which represent the "divine family" of Shiva, Parvati, Ganesha and Skanda always include Nandi: according to legend, the bull was given to Shiva and Parvati as a wedding present from Daksha, Shiva's father-in-law.

Nandi shares many of his master's attributes: he is strong, fierce and sexually potent and is an embodiment of the power that can be attained by the taming of brute strength and by the control of passion.

In some Hindu cities, such as Varanasi, sacred animals are allowed to roam freely.

THE COBRA

The antithetical nature of Shiva as creator and destroyer, ascetic and erotic, is shared by one of his most important attendant symbols, the cobra. The cobra is lethal, yet it adorns Shiva's neck as protection. Similarly, Shiva's son, Ganesha (see pp.72–3), is guarded by cobras about his ankles and his chest; and Murugan – originally a Tamil deity, but later identified as another of Shiva's sons (see pp.76–7) – rides a peacock with a cobra in its mouth. Cobras also guard the *linga*, the Shiva phallus.

A monolithic, seven-headed cobra guards a Shiva linga *at Lepakshi in Andhra Pradesh.*

who was overawed by the Buddha's powers of concentration. The serpent prince Dharanendra shields the Jain Fordmaker, Parshva, in his meditations, while in Vaishnavite myth, the great serpent Ananta protects Vishnu while he rests.

The cow in Hindu mythology has always represented fertility and abundance. As the complete provider, the cow is the incarnate form of the benign aspect of the Great Goddess, she who nourishes and sustains the life that emerges from her "infinite womb". More recently, the cow has come to stand for "Mother India", the mythical embodiment of the modern Indian state. Cows are allowed to roam freely through the streets and are considered sacred by the Hindus. Large white bulls that resemble the mythical Nandi are often honoured with elaborate funerals.

Snake deities are often represented as half-human and half-snake. Nagakals, or snake stones, are either placed beneath trees in villages and towns, or they are displayed on the walls of temples, as in this example from Karnataka, in order to bestow auspicious protection on all who come to worship.

Sadhus

The greatest congregation of sadhus *occurs at the Kumbha Mela at Allahabad every twelve years.*

Sadhus (yogis) follow a path of penance and austerity to attain enlightenment. Believing the world to be made by the creative force of *maya* (illusion), *sadhus* are renunciants, rejecting worldly attachments and a life of "action" to erase past *karma* (see pp.24–5) and so liberate themselves into the world of divine reality. The extreme austerity of some *sadhus* does not mark them as religious fanatics in India. They are a common sight on the country's roads, and renunciation can also be the "fourth stage" of asceticism – after bringing up a family – in an orthodox Hindu's life.

Many *sadhus* imitate the mythological life of Shiva, the greatest of all ascetics. They carry a symbolic trident and wear three stripes of ash upon their foreheads to represent Shiva's triple aspect and his ascetic quest to destroy the three impurities – selfishness, action with desire and *maya*. The ascetic's two-sided drum (*damaru*) represents the union of Shiva and Shakti, and by worshipping the *linga* (see pp.66–7) ascetics honour Shiva's manifest form. The saffron-coloured robes or loincloths worn by many *sadhus* signify that they have been symbolically washed in the fertile blood of Parvati, Shiva's consort. Their presence at many of the sites of Shaivite myth confirms their devotion to this god.

Sadhus usually spend the first years of renunciation with their gurus, or teachers, performing the selfless service of *karma* yoga. Traditionally,

A sadhu *posing for tourists outside the palace at Amber.*

sadhus shave their heads as a sign of renunciation and surrender to their gurus, to whom lifelong attachments are made. Once fully acquainted with the spiritual and yogic arts, they usually leave their gurus' protection to wander the roads and forests, never staying long in one place. At this stage, they let their hair grow long and matted. *Sadhus* believe that moving around keeps the body-mind alert, but that staying in one place leads to stagnation.

There are many different Shaivite sects. Aghoti ascetics are devotees of Bhairava, the wrathful manifestation of Shiva; they live in cremation grounds and use the top part of human skulls as begging bowls. The Danda *sadhus* give away almost all their possessions, retaining only a waterpot, a loincloth and a staff. They subsist on the food that is given to them, eating it from their hands.

A typical emblem held by sadhus *is the* damaru *(left), the drum of Shiva, which is rattled to announce their arrival and departure from a village.*

PENANCE

A sadhu *buries his head in the sand as a form of penance.*

The largest number of *sadhus* belongs to the Juna Akhara sect, famous for the extremity of its penance and the yogic accomplishments of its *sadhus*. Penances, such as standing on one leg or holding one arm in the air for twelve years, are said to have lent the Akharas considerable powers (*siddhis*), such as lightness or levitation, invisibility and the ability to grow or shrink to any size. Many members of the sect perform penances such as burying their heads in the ground for several days at a time in order to attract alms from passers-by.

The first act of a sadhu *on arrival at a new site is to build a* dhuni *or sacred fire. A trident (right) is driven into the edge of the hearth in memory of Shiva sanctifying the fire. It is kept clean because it is believed to possess considerable power. The trident illustrated here is typical of those used by* sadhus *throughout India.*

Ganesha

The elephant-headed deity Ganesha is Hinduism's Lord of Beginnings, and the benign Remover of Obstacles. His animal mount is the rat, famed for its slyness, and his immense popularity is based as much on his trickery as on his ever-jovial willingness to solve the problems of his devotees. A typical tale of his light-hearted cunning involves a race around the world between the pot-bellied Ganesha and his fleet-footed brother, Skanda. Skanda set off in full flight on his peacock mount, while Ganesha claimed victory by simply walking around his divine parents, thus encircling the entirety of the universe.

Ganesha's image may originate from a tribal animal totem; the tales of how he acquired his animal's head are often seen as reflecting the assimilation of his tribal cult into mainstream Hinduism. He is now worshipped as a son of Shiva, yet legend has it that Shiva was not his

A wall painting of Ganesha in Jaipur.

A four-headed Ganesha riding a lion, from southern India.

true father. The most common account of his birth is that while Parvati was washing herself, she took some dirt and unguent from her leg to form a small model of a man. She gave life to the fig-

GANESHA'S ATTRIBUTES

Ganesha inherits hints of Shiva's asceticism: a cobra is coiled around his belly, and sprouts of matted hair suggest the dreadlocks of the Lord of Yoga. He is, however, too playful to be a serious ascetic. His attributes are an elephant goad, a noose and the bowl of sweetmeats eternally lifted to his mouth.

He is often depicted with one hand held upright in the gesture of fearlessness.

Ganesha is also the patron of letters and learning: the broken tusk that he holds in one of his hands was used as a stylus to write down later sections of the *Mahabharata* epic (see pp.56–7).

A painted plaster image of Ganesha carried in procession.

Ganesha's birth is celebrated by the Ganesh Chaturthi festival on the fourth day (*chaturthi*) of the lunar month Bhadrapada (August–September). In the state of Maharashtra, and in its capital, Bombay, elaborate clay models of Ganesha are paraded through the streets. The festival has assumed massive proportions and is attended by thousands of local inhabitants.

ABOVE *Positioned at the entrance to a temple, Ganesha is worshipped by devotees for his power to remove obstacles, thereby ensuring success in personal and business ventures.*

RIGHT *Small images of Ganesha are mass-produced for homes.*

ure, instructing him to guard the door while she bathed. Her husband, Shiva, returned to find a strange man-god in his house, and when he tried to pass through the door, Ganesha refused him entry. Furious, Shiva cut off the intruder's head, only to find that he had killed Parvati's own son. Shiva dispatched his *ganas* (attendant demons and dwarfs) to bring back the head of the first creature they met; they returned with the head of an elephant. Shiva placed this on Ganesha's shoulders and brought him back to life. He was welcomed into the divine family, and honoured with the title Ganesha or Ganapati, Lord of Shiva's *ganas*.

Ganesha's courage while defending Parvati's door has made him the guardian of entrances and Lord of New Openings. His image is often found on entrances to temples and homes; his name is invoked at the beginning of worship and when a new journey or project is planned. Weddings are blessed by Ganesha, as are other beginnings such as the New Year, and his image is often seen on calendars.

Shiva and Parvati

Shiva is both destroyer and creator, god of asceticism and of procreation. He is the Lord of Yoga, smeared with the ashes of renunciation and the cremation ground, yet he is also the source of the Ganges, the river that gives life. In spite of the multiplicity of forms in which he appears, Shiva is mostly worshipped through the *linga* (see pp.66–7), the symbolic, semi-abstract representation of the phallus.

Whereas many Hindu deities stand for specific attributes of divinity (*brahman*), Shiva remains a paradox – he is definable only by the oppositions that he embodies. The Pashupata sect, who worshipped him in the early centuries AD, deliberately performed seemingly nonsensical or indecent actions, such as going naked, dwelling in cremation grounds, or substituting faeces for

Shiva and Parvati are frequently represented in popular art, as in this 20th-century poster.

Bhairava, the ferocious aspect of Shiva, is shown here astride the corpse of Daksha, Shiva's father-in-law, from an 18th-century painting.

DAKSHA'S SACRIFICE

One famous Shaivite legend concerns Shiva's love for Sati, the daughter of Daksha. Shiva and Sati tricked Daksha into consenting to their marriage. But Daksha was disgusted by the ash-smeared body and matted hair of the ascetic god, and when he held a feast and fire sacrifice, he did not invite Sati and Shiva to attend. When Sati learned of her father's distaste for Shiva, she threw herself onto the sacrificial fire (see p.127). On hearing news of this, the enraged Shiva created Kali and Bhairava to kill Daksha

and wreck the sacrifice. He took Sati's miraculously preserved corpse from the fire and carried it for many years until it finally fell apart. Sati reincarnated herself as Parvati, "Daughter of the Himalayas", and resolved to join Shiva again, who was still lost in mourning. Kama, the Lord of Desire, fired an arrow of love at the god's heart, but Shiva, who had been meditating, was furious at the interruption. Opening his fearsome third eye, he burned Kama to ashes, but later, realizing that Sita had been reborn, Shiva longed for, and finally obtained, their reunion.

flowers on Shiva's altars. The aim of these acts was to reveal the illusory nature of opposites, thus demonstrating the underlying unity of the god's nature. Polarity is the work of *maya* (see pp.130–31) in Shaivite thought, and oppositions such as creation and destruction, and life and death, are understood to be mutually dependent. Such dualities form the basis of what is commonly called "reality".

In recognizing Shiva as a total, all-encompassing deity, Shaivite cults began to incorporate key aspects of goddess worship into their mythology. Shiva's power (*shakti*) was increasingly represented by his consort, a form of the goddess Devi (see pp.78–9). Like the mother goddess of old (see pp.20–21), Devi has both benign and horrific incarnations. She is the peaceful Sati, Uma or Parvati; her ferocious aspects manifest themselves variously as Chamunda, Kali and Durga (see pp.80–81). While Kali and Durga appear briefly to wreak destruction on Shiva's enemies, Parvati is always by his side, his perfect complement and celestial "wife". The sexual and spiritual union of Shiva and Parvati became the basis of Tantric and Shakta philosophy (see pp.110–11), and numerous legends describe the "divine family" at their home on Mount Kailasa.

ABOVE *Shaivite imagery pervades everyday life, as shown in this wall painting from Rajasthan.*

RIGHT *A modern temple in Hyderabad depicting the "divine family" – Shiva, Parvati and their son Ganesha – with the reclining bull, Nandi, also considered sacred, in the foreground.*

PARVATI VALLEY

Parvati Valley, near Kulu in Himachal Pradesh, is the setting of many of the myths that describe the life of Shiva and Parvati. At the foot of the valley are the hot springs at Manikaran. Legend has it that after making love with Parvati for 10,000 years, Shiva spent a further 10,000 years in meditation at Manikaran. His time there passed well, and in gratitude he made the rocks hot so that future yogis who visited the site would be able to sit there in warmth and comfort.

The name "Manikaran" is derived from a story in which Parvati lost a jewel (*mani*) in the river – it was later returned to him by the Lord of the Underworld in a cascade of hot water.

Southern sons of Shiva

In the southern Indian states of Tamil Nadu and Kerala, the gods Ayyappan and Murugan, the southern sons of Shiva, are worshipped as incarnate manifestations of Shiva's *shakti* (power), in much the same way as Vaishnavites honour *avatars* such as Krishna and Rama as incarnations of Vishnu. The myths recounting the lives of Ayyappan and Murugan are much influenced by the *bhakti* (devotional) movement (see pp.58–9), and are rooted in the local areas in which each cult is based. They are mainly worshipped as protectors of the village, and most stories relating to them tell of battles against local demons and the darkness of the forest. Both deities are represented as young and victorious; unlike the distant and transcendent Shiva, both are believed to play an active role in the lives of their devotees.

Murugan is the major deity of the ancient Tamils, and is still popular in modern Tamil Nadu as a "clan" or family god. Until this century, worship of Ayyappan was confined to Kerala, specifically to the mountain rain forests close to the Pamba river which forms the border with Tamil Nadu. In 1950, just 1,000 pilgrims travelled to Sabarimala, the jungle temple where Ayyappan is said to reside, while 400,000 made the journey in 1988. His origins are exclusively local, for he is a village god who slays the forest demons, but his devotees now also come from Madras, Bombay and Calcutta. To these pilgrims, Ayyappan is a symbol of change, development and ultimate success in the secular as well as spiritual world. Eighteen gold steps ascend from the forest to the entrance of Sabarimala temple, representing a ladder leading to moral and spiritual success. Each step stands for a different *raga* (vice or sin), and every year that a pilgrim climbs the steps another vice should be renounced. In this way the staircase comes to symbolize the devotee's own quest for spiritual release, the process of *jayikkuka* (becoming victorious) for which Ayyappan is renowned.

MURUGAN

Murugan is a popular rural deity in the foothills of western Tamil Nadu. He is often identified with Skanda, Shiva's warrior-god son, and like his northern counterpart he is usually shown carrying a spear or trident. Murugan may have originated as a fertility god and his worship probably included some form of orgiastic dancing.

Murugan, accompanied by a peacock on which he rides, as shown in a modern poster.

Pilgrims to Sabarimala decorate the buses and cars in which they travel with images of Ayyappan.

THE STORY OF AYYAPPAN

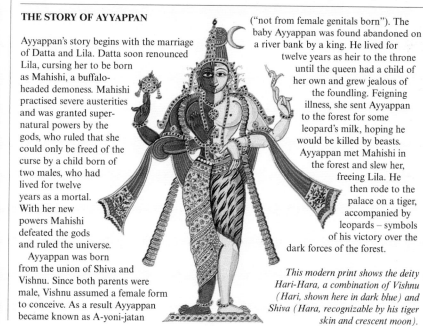

Ayyappan's story begins with the marriage of Datta and Lila. Datta soon renounced Lila, cursing her to be born as Mahishi, a buffalo-headed demoness. Mahishi practised severe austerities and was granted supernatural powers by the gods, who ruled that she could only be freed of the curse by a child born of two males, who had lived for twelve years as a mortal. With her new powers Mahishi defeated the gods and ruled the universe.

Ayyappan was born from the union of Shiva and Vishnu. Since both parents were male, Vishnu assumed a female form to conceive. As a result Ayyappan became known as A-yoni-jatan ("not from female genitals born"). The baby Ayyappan was found abandoned on a river bank by a king. He lived for twelve years as heir to the throne until the queen had a child of her own and grew jealous of the foundling. Feigning illness, she sent Ayyappan to the forest for some leopard's milk, hoping he would be killed by beasts. Ayyappan met Mahishi in the forest and slew her, freeing Lila. He then rode to the palace on a tiger, accompanied by leopards – symbols of his victory over the dark forces of the forest.

This modern print shows the deity Hari-Hara, a combination of Vishnu (Hari, shown here in dark blue) and Shiva (Hara, recognizable by his tiger skin and crescent moon).

Devi

The oldest and most frequently manifested deity of the Hindu pantheon is Devi, the Goddess. Like the ancient pre-Aryan mother goddess (see pp.20–21), Devi appears as both the broad-hipped provider and as the fierce destroyer of mortal life. She is worshipped in India's villages in myriad forms, such as Bhu, the ancient earth goddess, Parvati, daughter of the Himalayas (see pp.74–5), the avengers Kali and Durga (see pp.80–81), and as the consort of numerous male gods. She is often called Mother – *Mata* or *Mataji* in northern India, and *Amman* in the jungles of the south – and is usually represented as the *yoni*, the female principle surrounding the male *linga* (see pp.66–7).

Like the old mother goddess, Devi is primarily associated with fertility and the earth. India itself is seen as the body of Devi, whose forms can be found in the features of the landscape. Cities such as Calcutta (*Kali Ghat*) draw their names from forms of Devi, and goddesses are often named after natural features, such as Rama's consort, Sita (see p.53), whose name means furrow. Where the male deities of the Hindu pantheon are otherworldly, the *avatars* of the goddess are active and immanent. Devi is not distant from the *maya* (illusion) of worldly life (see pp.130–31), but is known as *Mahamaya* (Great Illusion). Since the land itself is her body, she may be both known and approached by her devotees.

The male deities Shiva, Brahma and Vishnu (the *trimurti*) embody ideals toward which their devotees can only strive. Brahma is little more than a transcendent principle; Vishnu represents a moral ideal of inhuman purity; Shiva's ascetic severity is unattainable by mortals. The Goddess, on the other hand, is defined by her action in this world. While Shiva meditates high in his Himalayan retreat, the Goddess in her incarnation as Kali fights on the

CHINNAMASTA

Chinnamasta, the Goddess of Great Wisdom, has been a popular Hindu deity since the 12th century. She is usually depicted standing on the back of Rati, who is copulating in the superior position with Rati's husband Kama, the Lord of Desire. The energy generated by this sexual intercourse feeds Chinnamasta, who in turn decapitates herself to nourish her devotees with her own blood, thus uniting sex and death – the opposite but interconnected principles which govern the universe.

In this mid-19th-century Tantric image, the goddess Chinnamasta stands on the yoni *triangle representing the feminine cosmic principle. Her blood feeds two* yoginis, *Tantric symbols of the left and right sides of the body.*

battlefield, slaying the demons of ignorance with a vigour quite unlike Krishna's calm detachment (see pp.60–61). The Goddess's power to act in the human world was elaborated by theologians, particularly in the group of texts called the *Tantras* (see pp.110–11). They recognized Devi as the holder and centre of divine power (*shakti*). The Goddess's horrific forms, such as Kali and Durga, were worshipped through Tantric rituals as supreme powers in themselves, unfettered by transcendent male divinities.

The Saptamatrikas, *or Seven Mothers, embodying the energies of all the major gods of Hinduism, usually appear together with Kali, as in this 9th-century relief from central India.*

LAKSHMI

Lakshmi is the goddess of wealth and plenty. She is the consort of Vishnu (see pp.50–51). Whereas Vishnu stands for the transcendent moral good and order (*dharma*) of the universe, Lakshmi represents all the good things in worldly life. She brings vitally needed rains (symbolized by her attendant elephants) and gold coins pour from her outstretched hand. She is worshipped throughout India as the goddess of good luck and good fortune.

GANGA

As well as being associated with the land, Devi is linked with India's great rivers, many of which are worshipped as divine forces in themselves. The river Ganges, for example, is characterized in the Hindu pantheon as Ganga, the goddess who resides in the infinite folds of Shiva's matted hair. Rural goddesses are often worshipped by throwing garlands of flowers into rivers just as temple icons are worshipped by placing flowers around their heads.

A dry-mud image of Devi being prepared for worship in Calcutta.

Durga and Kali

Durga is a manifestation of Devi (see pp.78–9) and is widely worshipped as the terrible aspect of the benign goddess Parvati, daughter of the Himalayas (see pp.74–5). But whereas Parvati acts only as Shiva's consort, Durga exists in her own right, slaying the demons of ignorance with the power (*shakti*) of her own ferocity.

Since the first centuries AD, Durga has been revered throughout India for slaying the buffalo-demon Mahishasura. The story, drawn from the *Durga Charitra* ("Exploits of the Great Goddess Durga"), is one of the most famous of Hindu

myths. The great demon Mahishasura practised such severe austerities that the gods were forced to grant him near-infinite power. He took the form of a buffalo and railed against the gates of the heavens. The furious gods, overwhelmed by the demon's tremendous might and the *arita* (disorder) ensuing from it, created Durga, combining their power in a single deity. The mighty goddess annihilated hordes of demon armies and finally slew Mahishasura by placing her foot upon his neck and decapitating him.

The head of the goddess Durga in a Durga Puja procession.

DURGA PUJA

The Durga Puja is the most popular and elaborate religious festival celebrated in Bengal. Devotees of Durga undergo a nine-day fast. Family members are encouraged to return to their ancestral homes. On the last day of the festival huge images of Durga are carried through the streets and taken to a river where they are ceremoniously immersed. At the end of the Puja, married daughters must return to the houses of their husbands, evoking the myth of the benign goddess Parvati returning to Mount Kailasa, the abode of Shiva.

Durga riding the lion that battles with the buffalo-demon Mahishasura is a recurring theme in Indian art. The goddess is frequently shown armed with the divine weapons of the gods, and her composure is in striking contrast to the violent posture of Mahishasura. In this 18th-century miniature, the demon takes human form, except for his fierce, animal-like head. Here, uncharacteristically, he is shown riding a horse and brandishing a European gun.

This 17th-century miniature painting from northern India depicts Kali slaying demons.

Kali, "the black one", is the destroyer, the fearsome goddess with the long red tongue. Her enemies are devoured by her cavernous mouth; her eyes are bloodshot with the desire for battle and carnage, and a garland of skulls hangs around her neck.

Kali's image is the most terrifying of all Hindu deities, yet she is adored as much as feared by her devotees. The poets and scholars of 18th- and 19th-century India, such as Ramprasad Sen and Ramakrishna, worshipped her as "the holy mother", and the earlier Tantric cults saw in her the supreme power of godhead.

Like Shiva, Kali is an outsider, feared and appeased by the other gods. Both Kali and Shiva live in cremation grounds, for they are outcasts. Unlike Shiva, lost in meditation, Kali rampages on the battlefields of worldly life.

KALI BESTRIDING SHIVA

One of the most popular images of Kali depicts her bestriding the sleeping, or "corpse", form of the god Shiva. Tantric images represent her in the act of sexual intercourse, squatting upon Shiva's prostrate body. Such images are symbolic of the union of Shiva and Shakti, the male and female principles of godhead.

The fearsome goddess Kali is depicted (left) in a popular print bestriding Shiva's body, and (right) in a far less frightening pose in an 11th-century bronze statue.

THE THUGS

The Thugs (*Sthagas,* or cheats) were organized bands of assassins, who terrorized travellers across India for more than 300 years. A Thug would befriend a single traveller and then strangle him, claiming to do so in Kali's name. They were suppressed under British rule during the 1830s, and today only their name survives.

Yogic Arts

Yoga is a practical path to self-realization, a means of attaining enlightenment by purifying the entire being, so that the mind-body can experience the absolute reality underlying the illusions of everyday life. It is one of the most famous of Hinduism's philosophical traditions, now practised by Hindus, Christians, agnostics and atheists alike.

Yoga is less a religion than a mode of spiritual progress, in which bodily discipline influences consciousness, and concentrating the mind gives the adept mastery over matter. Simple exercises are said to lend the adept "yogic powers", such as levitation, for which yoga is renowned. Advanced yogis claim to possess extraordinary powers, such as the ability to disappear at will, but they do not generally use them in public.

Whereas Raja Yoga rejects the body as an illusion, Hatha Yoga uses it as a method of liberation. Hatha yogis practise "the yoga of force" to discipline and purify the body so that they can construct a new "subtle" body that is immune to *karma* and disease. Once purified, the subtle body-mind attains the ecstatic state of *samadhi*, and intensive meditation then leads it to release. Kundalini Yoga seeks the union of Shiva and Shakti within the adept's subtle body by drawing the "serpent" of immanent female power up to the energy centre at the top of the head, the location of transcendent godhead.

Yoga has different methods of uniting the self with the godhead (brahman). An adept of Raja Yoga – which emphasizes knowledge (jnana) and devotion (bhakti) as paths to release – is depicted in this 16th-century miniature.

Yoga

A 7th-century relief at Mamallapuram shows the god Shiva granting a boon to the sage Bhagivathi, who is standing in a yoga position on one leg.

Yoga is the science and praxis of obtaining liberation (*moksha*) from the material world. Like Buddhism and Jainism, it not only points the way to release, but offers a practical means of arriving there. The yoga that is famous in the West today is the Hatha Yoga (see pp.88–9) of bodily positions (*asanas*); this is only a small branch of yoga, however, whose diverse philosophies and forms of liberation constitute one of the traditional six systems of Indian thought. Bodily *asanas* are a means of purifying and then recreating the body so that it can be used as a tool to achieve release from *maya*, the world of illusion (see pp.130–31).

Although yoga is most often taken to mean "union", a more literal equivalent is the English word "yoke". The yogi strives to "yoke" the Lower Consciousness (what we now call the ego) to the Supreme Consciousness of the Absolute. Self-control, asceticism and meditation then discipline the body-mind so that it can be "fitted" to the higher reality of *brahman* (godhead). Enlightenment is not so much "experienced" by the body-mind as "witnessed" by a consciousness that is now "awake", or "yoked" to the real nature of the world.

To yoke himself or herself to the higher truth, the yogi's prime aim is disentanglement from the binds of *maya* by an ascetic process of detachment and sensory suppression. This world of *maya* is likened to the surface of a lake blown by the wind. When the wind is stilled, the broken images and continual flux on the surface of the lake are shown in fact to reveal true forms, solid and constant like the permanence of absolute godhead. Similarly, yoga aims to still the wandering and flux of consciousness that fills the mind with continually changing perceptions and thoughts. When a beginner attempts even the most basic yogic exercise, such as concentrating on a single point or on the breath, the mind soon begins to wander, distracting the practitioner with imaginary conversations, memories and random thoughts.

Yoga emerges from a dualistic philosophy which postulates that matter (*prakriti*) and spirit (*purusha*) are fundamentally separate entities, and that the spirit is bound in matter, and thus in *maya*, by the moral history of its individual *karma* (past actions). Accordingly, we are continually reborn in the endless round of *samsara* (rebirth) because we have to experience the consequences of our *karma*. Desire is the cause of every action, and it is the desire to act and live fruitfully in this world that the yogi must first eliminate if he or she is to eradicate the consequences of past actions and prevent new *karma* from accumulating.

The more esoteric types of yogic thought are possibly derived from the Indian shamanism that predated the coming of the Aryans (see pp.12–13). Yoga can use shamanistic techniques to induce trance and possession, and believes in an "inner heat" (*tapas*) that can "burn off" the coils of worldly reality. But whereas shamanism aims always to gain control over the powers or deities of the universe, the yogi strives to transcend these powers and reach a reality beyond even the gods.

SHIVA, LORD OF YOGA

A modern print showing Shiva seated in a yoga posture in the mountain heights of Kailasa.

Shiva is Hinduism's Lord of Yoga. He is often depicted seated in the *padmasana* (lotus), *siddhasana* (master) or *sukhasana* (comfortable) yogic postures, his concentration (*dharana*) fixed in meditation upon the experience of "pure consciousness". Central to Shaivite philosophy is his paradoxical nature as an erotic ascetic: the greatest of all ascetics, he is at the same time the god of the *linga* (phallus). His image thus embodies the Tantric (see pp.110–11) and Hatha Yogic synthesis of yoga and *bhoga* (sexual enjoyment) that aims to transcend the limits of the material world. Shiva Yoga is therefore non-dualist: it does not postulate an absolute distinction between soul and body, but attempts to generate a yogic "inner heat" within the physical body to transform it into a subtle body capable of enlightenment. In the *Shiva-Purana*, yoga is defined as the restraint of all activity other than meditation upon Shiva as "pure consciousness".

The first Vedic mention of yoga is in the *Katha Upanishad*, where it is likened to a chariot in which the reasoning consciousness is the driver, and the body is the cart. Mastery of the body is thus achieved by control of the senses. This text is an early example of the basic yogic belief that the mind and body are not inherently separate but linked – that bodily austerity can influence consciousness, and that control over the senses can give mastery over *prakriti* (matter). This idea was developed by Hatha Yoga and by yogic methods involving the concept of Kundalini (see pp.94–5) in the technique of *pranayama* (breath control), whereby the higher and lower consciousnesses were said to be animated by the same vital force (*prana*).

An adept practising yoga on the banks of the sacred river Ganges at Varanasi.

The *Bhagavad Gita* (see pp.60–61) is sometimes described as being in some sense a book of yoga. It emphasizes self-discipline and control over the senses as essential techniques of a yoga that it defines as the "balance" of the individual and universal consciousness. "The wavering, restless mind goes wandering on," Krishna advises the despondent Arjuna: "you must draw it back, and have it focused every time on the soul ... Yoga is a harmony," he later continues, "a harmony in eating and resting, in sleeping and keeping awake: a perfection in whatever one does."

The yoga that Krishna expounds in the *Bhagavad Gita* is the *karma* (action) yoga of self-control, and *bhakti* yoga – the way of "devotion". *Bhakti* (see pp.58–9) is essentially a theistic doctrine, imagining a separate, personal and active deity who can be reached by the power of the devotee's love and yearning. Rather than striving to escape from the illusory world of ordinary reality, the *bhakti* yogis embraced it, seeing everywhere the manifest glory of the god they worship. Krishna makes *bhakti* the highest form of yogic discipline. "Of all the yogis, those who worship me fervently, self-lost in love, come closest to my heart, attuned to me."

The form of yoga that is known in the West today was first elaborated in the *Yoga Sutra* attributed to Patanjali. Some scholars maintain that this text was written as early as the 2nd century BC, but it was probably formulated at a later date. The original text comprises only 195 brief sentences or aphorisms; a mass of later commentaries has been added through the centuries. Of these, the *Yoga-bhashya* (*Elucidation of Yoga*) is said to have been composed by the legendary sage Vyasa in *c*.AD500, and the *Tattva-vaisharadi* (*Science of Reality*) of Vahaspati Mishra was probably added as late as *c*.AD850.

The system of thought in the *Yoga Sutra* is dualistic, with Patanjali outlining a path to a liberation (*kaivalya*) that involves a fundamental detachment of the individual soul from the world of matter, and also from other souls. His method of escape is mental concentration – the gradual withdrawal of attention from worldly experience, and its diversion toward a permanent non-illusory consciousness (*purusha*) within.

EIGHT LIMBS OF RAJA YOGA

There are eight "limbs" to Patanjali's Raja Yoga (Royal Yoga). The first five deal with training the body and the last three teach the perfection of the self. *Yama* and *niyama* form the ethical core of the discipline.

Yama (self-control or restraint) regulates the yogi's external activities, and is based upon the five moral rules of non-violence, truthfulness, not stealing, chastity and non-acquisitiveness.

Niyama (observance) lists five regulations governing personal behaviour: purity, contentment, austerity, the study of scripture and devotion.

Asana (posture) suggests that the yogi should be seated in certain positions when meditating. The many *asanas* that are familiar to Western practitioners of yoga are not mentioned in the *Yoga Sutra*, which simply advises the yogi to find a suitable position so that he or she remains comfortable and is not disturbed.

Pranayama (breath control) is the most basic yogic technique. It is said that by controlling the breath the yogi can control both the body and the mind.

Pratyahara (inhibition) is the withdrawal of the senses from their objects, thus eliminating contact with the material world that binds the individual soul to *samsara* (rebirth). "As the tortoise retracts its limbs into the middle of the body," says one yoga text, "so the yogi should withdraw the senses into himself."

Dharana (concentration) is thought without the aid of the senses; it precedes meditation and involves the gathering of psychic energy through intense concentration upon an internal image, whether this be a deity, *mandala*, or any other object.

Dhyana (meditation) is a deepening of concentration until consciousness becomes a "one-directional flow" toward a single inner object.

Samadhi (ecstasy) is a trance in which the yogi is no longer even conscious of meditating. It is "the perfect forgetting of [the] meditation" that precedes it. In this ecstatic state the distinction between the meditating subject and the object is lost, the individual consciousness being transformed into full awareness of the universal Self.

This miniature painting illustrates the principal asana *(posture) of Raja Yoga.*

Hatha Yoga

The aim of Hatha Yoga ("Yoga of Force") is to make the body a worthwhile receptacle for self-realization. For this reason, it is the most physical of all the yogic paths. Rather than rejecting the body as a useless tool of *maya* (illusion; see pp.130–31), Hatha Yoga embraces it as the instrument of release. Hatha yogis see no distinction between lower and higher consciousness, or between the body and the mind, but perceive them all as manifestations of the same "life force" (*prana*).

The physical prowess vital to all yogic disciplines becomes paramount in Hatha Yoga, which employs an astonishing array of physical exercises to harness and manipulate the life force. These primarily involve the use of bodily postures (*asanas*), mental

A page from an 18th-century yogic textbook illustrating various asanas *(postures) and mudras (gestures).*

concentration and breath control (*pranayama*). The discipline has generally been rejected by the more orthodox schools of Hinduism, which point to its "body magic" and the apparent acquisition of supernatural powers as evidence of spiritual decadence. This has not lessened its influence, however, and the practical bodily exercises and methods of mental training it employs have in recent years become by far the most popular yogic techniques in the West.

Hatha Yoga was first propagated by the Kanpatha sect whose founder was the 10th-century ascetic Gorakhnatha, also the most important guru of the Natha *sadhus* (see pp.70–71). The Kanpatha and Natha *siddhas* (yogic masters) sought liberation by alchemically transforming the body into a "subtle" yogic body immune to *karma* and disease, and endowed with supernatural powers. Physical exercises such as breath control were utilized to encourage the flow of vital energy into the "central channel" (*sushumna nadi*) that leads from the bottom *chakra* (see p.95) at the base of the pelvis all the way up to the Thousand-petalled Lotus at the top of the head, the seat of Shiva, who is "pure consciousness".

Hatha Yoga places great emphasis on purificatory processes. The first level of attainment is the removal of disease in the body, after which the adept eliminates the *dosha* (impurities) that limit his or her further progress. A new "perfect" body is then made from the *soma* or *amrita* (nectar of immortality) that fills the top *chakra*. This divine elixir is said to drip down from the top *chakra* to be burnt away by the "flaming sun" at the bottom of the *sushumna* channel; by reversing this flow, adepts can burn away their ordinary body instead, and build a new immortal one from the overflowing nectar. The yogi then transforms his or her "perfect" body into a divine one, and thereby attains the state of godhead. He or she may then delight in the *lila* (play) of the creative power of *maya* (world illusion), changing shape at will while moving through the manifold forms of creation.

Practitioners of Hatha Yoga claim that their methods are the only way to achieve immortality. They believe that it is only through a "perfect" body that the individual soul can find release, and they reject not only the sacred Hindu scriptures but also the mind-orientated techniques of Raja Yoga (see pp.86–7).

This Hatha yogi is assuming the kukkuta *(cock) posture to harness the flow of prana (life force) in his "subtle" body.*

ASANAS

The most widely used manual on Hatha Yoga is the *Hatha Yoga Pradipika*, composed by Svatmarama in the 14th century AD. The *Pradipika* is essentially a practical guide to Hatha Yoga's core techniques, and it describes sixteen *asanas* (postures) suitable for meditation, most of which are based on the cross-legged "lotus position". *Asana* literally means "seat" and probably first referred to the surface on which a yogi sits to meditate. It has now come to mean the many positions outlined in modern yogic texts. The *Pradipika* describes the *asanas* in considerable detail, since they not only aid mental concentration but also cure a number of physical ailments and keep the body in good health.

CHRIST AS A YOGI

Legend has it that the missing years in the Biblical account of Christ's life were spent in Kashmir learning the arts of Hatha Yoga. Some Hindus, most of them Shaivite *sadhus*, maintain that Christ's mastery of illusion and apparently occult power derived from his training as a yogi. They cite his ability to walk on water and perform minor miracles, such as turning water into wine, as proof of his yogic prowess, seeing in his powers the *siddhis* (accomplishments) that are a by-product of yogic discipline (see pp.90–91). Above all it is the story of the crucifixion that has fuelled the myth of Christ as *siddha* (yogic master). The legend relates that Christ did not die on the cross, but (through breath control) stopped his heartbeat to simulate the physical condition of death. As in Hatha Yoga, he used his body as a metaphor for spiritual advancement, taking on it the sins of his devotees, which could then be burnt off by austerity. According to the legend, Christ re-animated himself after three days in deep trance and, after appearing briefly to his disciples, returned to Kashmir, where he later died.

Like Hindu deities, images of Christ, such as this one outside a church in Bombay, are garlanded with flowers.

Yogic Powers

Female adepts prepare to undertake the celebrated yogic art of walking on fire.

Hindu, Buddhist and Jain myth abounds with tales of holy men who have acquired the most extraordinary supernatural powers by the practice of asceticism. Ascetics have always been feared as much as respected in India for their seemingly magical powers, their ability to change shape, and the sureness of their curses.

Siddhis are "accomplishments" in the yogic arts, an adept of which is known as a *siddha* – a master not only of his or her own body and mind but also of the forces of nature. *Siddhis* are said to be by-products of yoga, and may appear after a relatively short time. The yogi should not strive to attain supernatural powers, but should accept them as a natural consequence of asceticism, and

as signs of "success". By recognizing that the world is *maya* (illusion), the yogi gains the creative power to manipulate it on the way to *mahasiddhi*, the "great accomplishment" that is *moksha* (release). "He who has conquered the senses", declares the *Yoga-Bija*, a well-known text, " ... can, by his own will, assume various shapes and make them vanish again".

The *Yoga Upanishads* acknowledge two classes of yogic powers: the *kalpita* (artificial) and the *akalpita* (non-artificial) *siddhis*. "Artificial" *siddhis* are transient, having only a temporary effect, and may be attained with relative ease, by using herbs, ritual, magic, *mantras*, or "elixirs". *Akalpita siddhis*, on the other hand, are derived from *svatantrya* (self-reliance): they are permanent and are recognized as the mark of a true adept.

A host of Indian stories describes determined yogis who can perform almost any feat. Legends have them prophesying the future, growing to the size of a mountain or shrinking to a grain of dust, producing fire from their bodies, assuming any form, even dissolving the universe with their power. Popular religion in India often associates yogis more with their powers than with their spiritual quest, but yogic texts themselves warn against the "temptation" of allowing *siddhis* to

Levitation exercises are part of yogic instruction at the Maharishi's ashram in the USA.

divert the adept from his or her path. Just as *maya* must be transcended, so must the powers of creative illusion. The *Yoga Upanishads* advise ascetics to keep their *siddhis* secret, because public display would disrupt a life of quietude, and may fill the individual self with a pride that could only bring *karmic* entanglement.

A legend relates that as the Buddha was walking by a river he met an ascetic performing austerities. The ascetic declared that by standing on one leg for forty years he had attained the power to walk on water, and so set off across the river. The Buddha was unimpressed and asked him what the purpose was of wasting forty years to walk on water when a ferry was moored at the bank. Like the Jain Fordmaker Mahavira (see p.42–3), the Buddha advised against the practice of yogic powers, declaring that rather than being an aid to contemplation, such *siddhis* were an obstacle in the renunciant's path. He did not condemn them outright, accepting that they may be useful as aids to concentration, but he condoned their use only if they led to "compassion" and to the alleviation of suffering.

A levitation demonstration in Sri Lanka: the chief performer is supported on a thin stick draped in white cloth.

LEVITATION

A levitating yogi is perhaps one of the most enduring images that the West has of India. *Laghiman* (levitation) is one of the eight "great powers", but yogic texts insist that its practice should remain secret so as to avoid corruption. It is described as the ability to become airborne like the tuft of a reed, and usually accompanies intensive exercises in breath control (*pranayama*).

THE MAHASIDDHIS

There are generally believed to be eight *mahasiddhis* (great powers) that accompany the path to release, which may be attained by a life of austerity and penances. The *mahasiddhis* are: the power to become small or invisible; the power to grow large (as large as the universe); the power to become light and so walk on water or levitate; the power to become as heavy as the world; the power of irresistible will; the power of "mastery"; the power of subjugating nature; and the power of fulfilment of all desires.

A yogi buries his head in the sand as a form of penance.

Prana

The literal meaning of *prana* is "breathing forth", but it is commonly taken to mean "life force" or a "vital energy" that permeates all beings. The practice of *pranayama* (breath control) attempts to "expand" this life energy and is said to rejuvenate the body-mind. It is believed that, ultimately, *pranayama* can lead to bodily immortality.

In texts of the *Vedas*, the word *prana* is used to denote a "universal life force" or "vibratory power", linking it to the Hindu idea that sound preceded the creation of the universe and that reality is held together by the vibration of the sacred syllable *Om* (see pp.108–9). In the *Upanishads*, *prana* is one of the most frequently used epithets for the *atman* (soul). Several passages examine the relationships between *prana* and the five organs of the "self" – speech, breath, sight, hearing and thought, which in turn correspond to the five natural forces – fire, wind, sun, moon and the four points of the compass.

Just as the *atman* is an inner spark of the outer *brahman* (godhead), with which it is identical, so *prana* is the life force both within and without. *Prana* is said to have five aspects variously located within the human body: the *prana* (ascending breath) pervades the region from the throat to the heart, and includes both inhalation and exhalation; the *apana* is located below the navel, strengthening the large intestine and helping with the excretion of waste; the *samana* is located between the heart and the navel, and controls digestion; the *udana* (up-breath) is between the throat and the brain, and is responsible for the face, eyes, ears, speech and brain, controlling access to higher states of consciousness; the *vyana* pervades the entire human body, coordinating energy flows and facilitating basic functions such as movement. *Prana* and *apana* sometimes refer to inhalation and exhalation respectively.

"Breath expansion" (*pranayama*) is the "fourth limb" of Patanjali's eight limbs of Raja Yoga which is laid out in the *Yoga Sutra* from the 2nd century BC (see p.86). It works by breath control, specifically by prolonging the duration of the withheld breath, which is said to prolong life. *Pranayama* is that which arouses the *kundalini* serpent (see pp.94–5), and it is said to strengthen and rejuvenate the body. Its most important function is to create a method through which the mind can be controlled. It is the most essential yogic technique – yoga without breath control is often likened to attempting to cross the ocean in an unbaked earthenware vessel.

There are three phases of *pranayama* – inhalation, retention and exhalation of breath through the left and right "channels" (*nadi*) in the nose. The left channel is the *ida nadi*. It is linked with the female, the moon, the colour red and death, and is thought to be "cooling". It influences the left side of the body and controls thought. The flow of breath through the right nostril is drawn through the *pingala nadi*. It is linked with the male, the colour white, the sun and life, and is believed to be "warming". It controls the right side of the body and regulates its *shakti* (energy) flows. The aim of *pranayama* is to balance the left and right channels. If this is achieved, it is thought to engender spiritual enlightenment and produce health, strength and longevity.

ENERGY CHANNELS

Each phase of breath stimulates a particular energy cluster within the human body. Once awakened, each cluster is said to transmit its own energy which may transform the body-mind of the adept. Destructive energy may be produced by over-concentration upon the *apana* breath. However, by diverting this energy "upward" to the heart and throat clusters, the negative and positive forces are united, and the body-mind made whole.

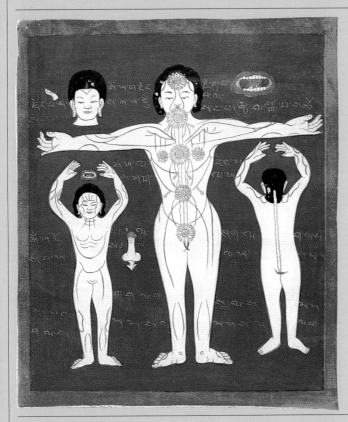

Figures in this modern painting, based on a Tibetan original, show the body's veins and centres of breath control. Harnessing the flow of energy through the breath channels is said to lead to four stages of yogic attainment: "perspiration", "trembling", "jumping like a frog" and "lightness" or "levitation".

THE FOUR REQUISITES

There are four requisites of successful *pranayama*. The first is "right place" (*sthana*), preferably somewhere quiet and cool, away from distractions; secondly, it must be the "right time" (*kala*), ideally the hours before dawn when the stomach is neither full nor empty. A beginner should only practise *pranayama* for five to ten minutes at a time, but a more advanced practitioner may take up to an hour. The third requisite is *mita-ahara* (right diet): this also includes "right posture" which should be the *padmasana* or *siddhasana* position. The seated body should be held erect with hands placed on the knees, and the eyes should be closed. The practitioner should start with "normal" breath and a thought-free mind. Lastly is *nadi-shuddhi*, the purity of the energy "channels" (*nadi*) through which the breath is "filled in" and "thrown out".

Kundalini

Kundalini (serpent) Yoga is an attempt to unite the two normally opposed principles of sexuality and spirituality by fusing their energies within an individual human body. In Tantric terms, these principles are *shiva* (the male principle), and *shakti* (the female principle). When united, they constitute the totality of Reality.

Shakti is thought of as a sleeping serpent (*kundalini*), which is coiled three-and-a-half, five or eight times about the lowest lotus (*muladhara*). It is found at the base of the pelvis exactly in the middle of the Four Fingers that can be placed between the anus and genitals. Its mouth is open over the Door to *Brahman* (the entrance to *sushumna*) with the central energy channel running up from the base of the spine to *sahasrara*, the highest energy centre located at the top of the head. It is here, in the Thousand-Petalled Lotus, that Shiva resides. The aim of Kundalini Yoga is to arouse the sleeping serpent, and then uncoil it by drawing it up the *sushumna* channel to the Thousand-Petalled Lotus which is "pure consciousness", thus uniting body and spirit.

The main technique employed by Kundalini *sadhakas* (adepts) is *pranayama* (see pp.92–3). The *sadhaka* should sit in a specified position (*asana*) and steady the mind by concentrating on the point between the eyebrows. By controlling the balance between the left and right breath channels (the *ida nadi* and *pingala nadi*), the adept creates an inner heat which rouses the serpent from its sleep.

*The coiled serpent (*kundalini*) is represented in this 19th-century illustrated Tantric manuscript, showing four of the meditative chakras.*

The *kundalini* is then drawn upward, and as its coils unfurl the apertures of the Door to *Brahman* are opened to allow access to the central channel. The rest of the body should then be devitalized by diverting *prana* (breath) away from the left and right channels to harness its full current into *sushumna*. The *ida* and *pingala* channels are then said to be dead, giving the *kundalini* serpent the power to uncoil. As it rises, each lotus blooms as if in welcome, and a flame descends to unite with the rising serpent. As the *kundalini* "pierces" each lotus, the energy of the lotus is "swallowed up" by the serpent and absorbed, leaving it in a state of *laya* (dissolution).

The *kundalini* energy fills the void and continues upward until it, too, is absorbed in the transcendent bliss of *sahasrara*. But the *kundalini* does not stay in the *sahasrara* for long: it is led back down the *sushumna* by its tendency to return to its original position. The adept should repeat the ascent and descent of the serpent, each time dwelling for longer in the *sahasrara*, only returning when so willed. When union is finally complete, the adept has attained liberation.

THE "KNOTS"

The ascent of the *kundalini* is hampered by a series of *granthis* (knots) where *maya shakti* (the power of worldly illusion) is particularly strong. These are often referred to as the *Tri-granthi*, the triple knots of Brahma, Vishnu and Rudra. These are placed at the abdominal, throat and lower head *chakras* respectively, blocking the *kundalini's* ascent to the crown *chakra* at the top of the head. Piercing these knots is said to be like forcing hot iron through the joints of a bamboo stick. The most difficult to pass is the abdominal knot, the piercing of which may involve considerable pain or disease.

THE CHAKRAS

Most Tantric schools propose that there are *chakras* (energy centres) ascending the central bodily channel, and that the seventh – *sahasrara*, the Thousand-Petalled Lotus in the head – unites the other six. Each is described as a lotus with varying colours and numbers of petals. At the base of the pelvis is the *muladhara chakra*, which is yellow, square and has four petals. The *svadhishthana chakra*, at the level of the genitals, is white, liquid and circular, with six petals. At the navel is the *manipura chakra*: red, incandescent and triangular, with eight petals. The *anahata chakra* is green, airy and located at the heart; it has twelve petals. At the throat is the sixteen-petalled *vishuddha chakra*: grey, ethereal and wisp-like. The *ajna chakra*, placed between the eyebrows, is depicted as a white two-petalled lotus signifying the union of male and female.

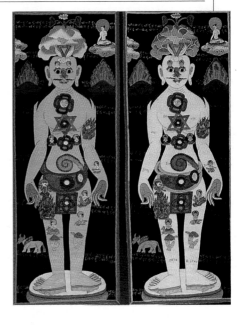

*Two examples of the Cosmic Man (*purusha*), indicating the bodily* chakras, *from an 18th-century painting in Nepalese style.*

Meditation

This 16th-century figure from Tamil Nadu shows a bearded sage seated in meditation.

Meditation (*dhyana*) is the means by which the purified body-mind reaches the deepest concentration or ecstasy (*samadhi*) and thence release to the ultimate goal and final limb of Raja Yoga (see p.87) in which the individual self is totally absorbed in the godhead. In Buddhism, intense visualization techniques, which are fundamental to all forms of yoga, have been raised to an unsurpassed level of sophistication. Only by "one-directional" concentration upon a single object is the mind stilled and the self annihilated.

Dhyana, the yoga of meditation, is the seventh of Patanjali's eight limbs of Raja Yoga. Through meditation, the body is first "perfected" and freed from the binds of *karma* (see pp.24–5) that

hold it in the cycle of rebirth. Once mastered, it ceases to distract the mind, which can then be fixed in meditation on the Absolute. The *Bhagavad Gita* (see pp.60–61) places the yoga of meditation above the scriptures and knowledge (*jnana*) as a path to liberation. "When your mind, which may be wavering in the contradictions of many scriptures, shall rest unshaken in divine contemplation," Krishna teaches, "then the goal of yoga is yours." The mind must first be stilled so that pure consciousness can "burn unflickering in a windless place". Here is Patanjali's sixth limb – concentration (*dharana*) – which must itself be transcended if the meditator is to lose awareness of the individual self.

Yogic texts dating from the 1st millennium AD differentiate between formal (*saguna*) and formless (*nirguna*) meditation. Formless meditation, the total absorption of the meditator into him- or herself, was considered too difficult for most practitioners. They were consequently taught the way of formal meditation, in which the adept focuses his or her attention on a specific object. This may either be an object of particular sacred significance such as a deity, a *mandala* or a *yantra* (see p.101), or it may be a simple object such as a stone or a leaf. The only objects which cannot be chosen as a focus for meditation are those which may arouse feelings of desire in the meditator.

The Boddhisattvas of Mahayana Buddhism (see pp. 38–9) are not gods, despite the worship their great images often receive, but resplendent objects of meditation, whose every detail is remembered and then visualized in the mind's eye. By deepening his or her concentration the adept then internalizes this object by visualizing it. The more complex Mahayana techniques take this to its greatest possible intensity, imagining every hair on a Boddhisattva's head until the inner image is as lucid as if it were seen with the outer eyes. When all distinction between the subject and object has gone, and the adept is no longer aware that he or she is meditating, the ecstatic state of *samadhi* is attained.

THE THREE OBSTACLES

There are said to be three kinds of thought that arise in the mind as "obstacles" to concentration.

Firstly is *Vichara*, the existential pondering in which the self poses unanswerable yet seemingly crucial questions such as "Who am I?" or "What is reality?". Secondly are *Vitarka*, the myriad negative thoughts that arise from experience. Patanjali recommended that these could be countered with "positive" states of mind such as compassion. Finally is *Viveka*, an awareness of and attachment to the dual nature of the world.

DHYANA ASANA

According to the teachers of *dhyana asana*, the place of meditation should be quiet, cool and free from distractions. After finding a comfortable spot, the adept should assume a basic sitting posture (*asana*): cross-legged with both knees touching the floor and with the spine held in a vertical position. The hands are then placed in the *dhyana mudra* ("seal of meditation") position in which the left hand is rested palm up on the folded legs and the right hand is placed on top, also palm up, with the thumb tips touching.

The peace and tranquillity of Gangotri on the upper Ganges make it a favoured site for meditation.

Tantric diagrams, such as this coloured mandala from an 18th-century manuscript, are used as aids in mind-focusing.

Mantras

"Om mani padme hum" *("Om! The jewel is in the lotus")* is *Buddhism's most powerful* mantra, *seen here painted on a wall in a Kathmandu street.*

The word *mantra* can be variously explained, but the root is in the Sanskrit verb *man* (to think). A *mantra* is a thought manifest in, or encapsulated by, a sacred utterance that possesses profound spiritual significance. Sound holds a key place in Hindu thought. Some writers believe that it preceded the creation of the universe, and its vibrations are thought to bind the atoms of the world. *Mantras* are sacred syllables that encapsulate particular forms of cosmic power (*shakti*). There are different forms of *mantra*, such as the "seed" (*bija*) *mantra*, which is thought to be an energy pervading both the human body and the universe. The deities are believed to be manifestations of *bija mantras*: Shiva, for example, is

linked with the mantra *"hrim"* and Kali is associated with the syllable *"krim"*.

A *mantra* need not possess verbal meaning; what is important is its sound. Complex *mantras*, which are built up from a series of sacred syllables, are often recited without an exact knowledge of what they signify. Many sacred Hindu texts, such as the *Vedas*, have been passed from generation to generation, at times orally, although not everyone understands the archaic Sanskrit in which they were composed. A devotee reciting the sacred syllables "absorbs" the power incorporated in the sound of the words. For example, the "root" *mantra "Om"* (see pp.108–9) is said to be the sound of vibration from which the universe was created.

By reciting it, the devotee partakes of the power of creation. *Om shakti* pervades the universe and, consequently, its sound as a *mantra* incorporates the entire range of human intonation, starting at the back of the mouth with the first element "A", passing through the sacred "humming" of the middle element, and ending in closed lips with the final "M".

If a guru feels that a devotee lacks the spiritual knowledge to attempt Hatha and Raja Yoga, he may suggest that the devotee first spend twelve years reciting sacred *mantras*. Mantra Yoga is said to be a gradual path to wisdom, on which the yogi can accumulate a host of *siddhis* (accomplishments). Many orthodox Hindus still see Mantra Yoga as a magical system which has origins in the intonations chanted by Vedic priests during sacrifices. These *brahmin* priests derived much authority from their claims to be able to summon the gods by uttering the correct sounds, thereby becoming more powerful than the gods themselves. Similarly, in Hinduism, the guru possesses knowledge of Mantra Yoga, and a *mantra* is useless to a student until a guru has ritually endowed it with power.

SOUND

There are generally believed to be four classes of sound (*shabda*): supreme sound (*para shabda*) is the most subtle of the four, and is the sound made by the base *chakra*; visible sound (*pashyanti shabda*) is associated with the heart and is manifested as the prime syllable *Om*; middle sound (*madhyama shabda*) incorporates the basic sounds of the Sanskrit alphabet and is the source of secondary *mantras*; manifest sound (*vaikhari shabda*) is the sound of human speech, and is considered the lowest of the four classes.

Walking to the right of a mani *wall, inscribed with a "jewel" mantra, is thought to generate the same power as reciting it.*

JAIN MANTRAS

The most famous Jain *mantra* is the *panchanamaskara* (the "five homages"), which is recited at almost every Jain ritual and spiritual event. Like the Jain universe, it is said to have no origin in time, and to possess no human author, but modern scholars generally attribute it to the 2nd century AD.

Unlike many of the Hindu *mantras*, the "five homages" has a specific meaning. It takes the form of five statements addressed to the five principal Jain ascetics, the *parameshthins* ("those who are situated on the highest plane"). The statements are: "Homage to the omniscient ones. Homage to the liberated. Homage to the teachers. Homage to the preceptors. Homage to all the monks of the world." This *mantra* is thought to produce extraordinary accomplish-ments (*siddhis*) – such as the ability to levitate and to fly – and to provide immunity from human and supernatural attack. Its recitation is believed to grant worldly success, to destroy pride and also to undermine the dominance of the self. Due to its capacity to "burn away" past *karma*, the *panchanamaskara* is believed to have a power equal to that gained by performing ascetic practices.

Mandalas

Mandalas are diagrammatic representations of the universe used in the Hindu and Buddhist traditions as aids to meditation and as part of sacred rituals. *Mandalas* may be painted on cloth or paper, fashioned out of wood or bronze, or drawn on the ground with coloured powders or threads, sometimes taking months to complete.

In Sanskrit, *mandala* means "circle", and the most important symbolic function of *mandalas* is as circular containers of "sacred space". At the centre of a *mandala* is a dot, or *bindu*, that represents Mount Meru (the mythical mountain at the centre of the universe) toward which the meditator "travels" on his or her path to enlightenment.

In Hindu thought, cosmic space is divided by a network of "power lines" that travel from north to south and west to east, charging the universe with the energy of godhead. These are represented within *mandalas* by intersecting triangles or squares, and the points of intersection, or spots, are considered to be particularly powerful. Hindu temples are built according to the structure of a *mandala*, with grid networks of intersecting architectural lines representing the cosmic power lines that create numerous architectural power spots.

To a Tantrist the most important and complex yantra *is the* Shri Yantra mandala. *Inside the outer square there are six concentric circles, enclosing nine intersecting triangles that symbolize the male and female divine energies. Five of the triangles point downward and are female, while the other four are male. The resulting pattern creates forty-three interlocking triangles, each of which is said to be the "house" of a Hindu or Tantric deity. There are usually two outer concentric circles of eight and sixteen lotus petals, and around the outside is a protective square known as the "world house". This painted example dating from the 18th century comes from Rajasthan.*

Symbolically, the "sacred space" within a *mandala* is a microcosm of the universe. By encircling that space, an adept aims to enclose the power (*shakti*) of the gods that it contains. It is also associated with the conscious space within, so that by meditating upon a *mandala* the individual may become merged with the cosmos.

Advanced yogis concentrate upon a *mandala* until they are able to internalize it. Once this has been achieved, they can visualize the *mandala* in their minds and merge with the cosmos that it represents. The yogi should then enter the *mandala*, following the lines of power that lead toward Mount Meru. On entering the sacred space within the *mandala*, the individual self is dissolved into the greater self, and then reintegrated into consciousness.

The Tantric movement (see pp.110–12) developed forms of the *mandala* called *yantras*. The *yantra* is a condensed symbol of the cosmos, an abstract pattern of lines and colours used for meditation. Enclosed in a square with four gates, like a wall surrounding a temple, there is a pictograph of the Tantric universe peopled by demons and deities whose multiplicity represents the subdivided *shakti* of the goddess. The goddess is symbolized by the triangles that in turn represent the *yoni* (vulva). The *yantra's bindu*, from which it "moves", stands for the goddess Tripura – the base of the universe – and for *bija*, the sacred seed.

JUNG

Jung wrote extensively about *mandalas*, and published several studies of the *mandala*-like patterns that emerged from the dreams and doodles of his patients. His interest led him to India, where he saw in the Tantric practice of the dissolution and reintegration of the self a process similar to his own theory of "individuation", in which the individual consciousness is united with the mythic content of the "collective unconscious".

ABOVE *Three of the stages in the development of the intricate* Shri Yantra mandala *showing the positioning of three downward and two upward pointing triangles which create a core for the final diagram.*

LEFT *A village woman preparing a* mandala *with nine seated goddesses arranged in lotus formation.*

Ritual and Performance

Ritual is the means by which the worshipper transcends worldly routine and enters into close contact with the *shakti* (power) of the gods. The special clothes, sounds, language and bodily movements employed in the performance of ritual serve to enhance its sacred significance.

Puja is the daily ritual by which devotees seek communion with the divine. Worshippers approaching the innermost sanctuaries of temples housing images of gods are met with explosions of colour and noise. Loud drumming and the dancing of ecstatic possession rituals are used to bombard the senses of the devotees of Amman, the mother goddess in rural southern India, so that their usual identity is obliterated and they are filled with the goddess's power.

Tantra is the most ritualistic of all Indian systems of thought. Tantric adepts use ritual to enhance their "realization" of an experience, stimulating their senses fully to transform their enjoyment into subtle energies that may be harnessed for "release" *(moksha)*. Tantric initiation may involve ritual sexual intercourse with a female "power holder" to unite the otherwise disparate energies of the male and female, mind and body, and the realms of the sacred and the profane.

These children are covering the floor of a temple with earth and leaves as a purification rite before the start of Holi, the Hindu spring festival celebrated on the day of the March full moon. Hindu restrictions on caste, sex and age are subverted during Holi, when the young can do as they want.

Puja

Devotees dancing in front of the ten-armed goddess Durga as part of the Durga Puja *festival.*

Puja is any Hindu ceremonial, from a simple ritual in the home to an elaborate public festival, in which images of the gods are worshipped. Its components vary from sect to sect and place to place but the *puja* is governed, at least theoretically, by rules in the *Shastras* and *Agamas* (sacred texts) and has probably changed little in 2,000 years.

In *Puja,* a deity, considered to be manifest in its image, is treated like a special guest. Elaborate ceremonies accompany the installation of a temple icon, governing how the image should be placed and how it should be dressed. It is first consecrated by the temple priests who chant *mantras* (see pp.98–9) and purify the image with incense and camphor. The priests then invite the deity to descend into its image, and finally they animate the icon with the rites of the infusion of breath and the opening of the eyes.

Many images of Vishnu and his *avatars* (see pp.50–51) depict the deity in human form, but the most common representation of Shiva is as the *linga*, a phallic symbol in the form of a short cylindrical pillar set in the *yoni*, a symbol of the cosmic vulva (see pp.66–7).

Puja is typically offered two or four times a day – at sunrise and sunset, and sometimes also at noon and midnight. The *pujari* (officiating priest) is responsible for the icon's well-being. He may perform *puja* alone, first purifying himself by washing in consecrated water before opening the door to the inner sanctuary. Temple musicians may beat drums and blow on large horns at this moment, or the *pujari* may simply ring a bell and clap

WORSHIP AT SABARIMALA

Most temple icons are said to house the power of a deity only temporarily, at the times when it is woken up at dawn and dusk. There are some temples, however, that are believed to be permanent dwelling places of the gods. These are characterized by especially elaborate *puja* ceremonies in honour of the residing god.

Sabarimala temple, in the middle of the rainforests bordering Kerala and Tamil Nadu in southwest India, is said to be the residence of the Hindu deity Ayyappan (see pp.76–7). Pilgrims walk all day through the forest wearing only a black *dhoti* (loincloth) and bearing an

Pilgrims going to Sabarimala temple bearing offerings in irrumudi *bags on their heads.*

irrumudi (a cloth bag with two sections) on their heads. Inside are two coconuts, one filled with ghee and the other unopened. The first is said to represent the soul within the outer shell of the coconut which bears the Three Eyes of Shiva. The second coconut stands for the self; on arrival at the temple the devotee smashes it on the bottom of eighteen golden steps, each standing for a different vice that has to be transcended before union with the deity can be achieved. Some devotees then perform the circumambulatory rite of *snanam pradakshina* to soak up Ayyappan's incarnate power. Wet from bathing, they roll three times around the inner circumference of the temple.

his hands to awaken the sleeping god. After asking its permission, the *pujari* washes an anthropomorphic statue, anoints it with oils, camphor and sandalwood paste, and dresses it with garlands and cloths.

A *linga* is washed with milk and water drawn from a sacred river such as the Ganges. As the liquid is poured onto the *linga*, it falls into the *yoni* at the base and runs out of a spout from which it is collected, now sanctified by contact with the deity. The *linga* is anointed with *ghee* (clarified butter) and sandalwood paste, and then decorated with flowers. In *arti* (light) *puja*, a metal dish with several burning wicks is

Whole and ghee-filled coconuts used in puja.

rotated in front of the *linga* and about the congregation who pass their hands over the flame to receive the *darshana* (blessing) of the deity. *Darshana* marks the climax of the ritual, when the fully awakened deity is displayed to devotees amid horn blasts, drumbeats and the swinging of balls of incense.

A devotee performs linga puja *by placing flowers on Shiva's emblems, the* linga *and* yoni, *newly wrapped in leaves and strewn with petals.*

Women in trance

Amman temples have no steps, walls or inner sanctums; they are usually placed on the village outskirts, under a sacred banyan tree or in a clearing in the scrub. Whereas the village deities tend to be depicted in human form, Amman is frequently represented by a simple stone icon in the shape of a mound or small menhir. On either side are icons of ancient snake gods. Ribbons and small black rings are often tied to the overhanging twigs and branches of a nearby tree.

In contrast to the predominantly male worshippers of the village gods, Amman's devotees are mostly female. Worship of the male village gods is characterized by rules and structure, but Amman is worshipped with ecstatic trance, abandonment and sacrifice. On highly auspicious days, such as the Friday following a full moon, she is offered chicken's blood by her devotees: more usually, she is left offerings of marijuana and betel (areca nut).

The role of women in religious festivals varies from the preparation of food (above) to performing puja *(right).*

Amman, the mother goddess of rural southern India (see pp.20–21), exhibits many of the traits typical of mother goddesses throughout the whole of India. As such she embodies the seemingly contradictory roles of life-giver and life-taker. As "mother" she is protective and benign, yet the villagers fear her anger and thirst for blood. Deities such as the heroic Ayyappan (see pp.76–7) represent the village, order and civilization; Amman, however, stands for the forest, chaos, danger and the primitive world of violence and sacrifice.

On festival days the village women themselves take marijuana, alcohol and betel to ease their way into ecstatic trance. An eyewitness gives a vivid description of just such a

A woman is shown here worshipping snake-stones that have been set beneath a tree and adorned with vermilion powder.

possession ritual: "The women then gathered around the Amman icon ... Temple drummers began to beat a rhythm that gradually accelerated and, after performing preparatory purification rituals, a *pujari* broke a coconut upon the stone.

"This signalled the onset of the ritual, the women began to dance, swaying drunkenly to the drums. Soon one was 'possessed by Amman', she danced as if in a daze. Some in the congregation touched the ground on which she had just trod to absorb some of the goddess's power. Others followed, whirling and stumbling, believing themselves to be possessed until, with a final beat of the drums, the dancing stopped. The women stood in silence and the *pujari* threw handfuls of water over them."

WOMEN AND SOCIETY

Some anthropologists claim that women enter trance as a means of access to a "public voice". Indian society has been male-dominated, and traditionally women have been relegated to subordinate positions in society and in the home. They nevertheless transcend the limitations of their social status by being possessed by a goddess who is not from within the village, but from outside, who represents the primeval forces of the forest.

At a festival in Kerala women jostle to touch one of their number who has been possessed.

AMMAN'S ICON

Local legend in Kerala tells how one day in the jungle village of Achenkovil a *pujari* went to give an offering to Amman. The goddess became angry and ate him, leaving only his hair and nails at the base of her icon, where they were found by a second *pujari*. The goddess's anger and hunger increased, and the terrified villagers sent for a famous ascetic, Tandri, who was wandering nearby. Tandri performed a yogic ceremony to calm Amman's anger; taking the stone icon, he turned it upside down, and after some time uprighted it. The yogi then split the icon in two. As the stone was believed to possess the goddess's full power, by splitting it the ascetic divided her power into two less potent portions.

Om

The shrines and walkway of the island temple of Omkaresvera are arranged in the shape of the Om *pictograph. This modern poster also shows (inset) the temple's* linga.

In Indian philosophy, matter is sometimes said to be created from sound and *Om* is the most sacred of all sounds, the syllable that preceded the universe and from which the gods were made. It is the "root" syllable (*mula mantra*), the cosmic vibration that holds together the atoms of the world and heavens. Therefore, all seemingly solid objects and living beings are manifestations of other primal sounds.

Since *Om* precedes all things, it is used as an invocation to prayer or sacred singing, and is often used as the final exclamation, in a way similar to the Jewish and Christian *Amen*. In yogic practice, *Om* is a fundamental part of the techniques of auditory meditation.

The *Om* is represented by a stylized pictograph (see far right), which appears throughout India on temple walls, election posters, and the fronts of buses and trucks. It is commonly used

During street processions celebrating the Hindu festival of Ramlila, a glittering cutout of Om *is used as a setting for the god Krishna and his favourite lover, Radha.*

as a symbol for religion itself, especially Hinduism, and may sometimes stand for the union of all creeds under the auspices of one god.

The *Mandukya Upanishad*, composed between 400BC and 200BC, is dedicated to an analysis of the theology and meaning of *Om*. The root syllable is described as the "bow" which fires the "arrow" of the self (*atman*) at the "target" of the absolute (*brahman*). In the *Maitrayaniya Upanishad*, *Om* is the "sound of the soundless absolute", the inherent form of transcendent cosmic energy.

The syllable *Om* is made up of four "quarters", the three phonetic elements (*a-u-m*) and a soundless fourth element. The first two represent the "pushing up" of the fire and light of the cosmic

THE TRIPUNDRAKA

The *tripundraka* are the three horizontal
stripes drawn across the head of Shiva. His
followers wear them to imitate and honour
him. They are usually made of ash or of
ground sandalwood paste, and are believed to
cool the brain while meditating. More
importantly, they represent the first three
elements of the syllable *Om*. Shiva also has
three eyes, the third of which is in the centre of
the *tripundraka*, and he carries a trident
(*trishula*). He is also
associated with the moon,
which rests in his matted
hair. The moon has three phases
(waxing, full and waning) and is
energized by its fourth aspect, *Om*,
the primal sound.

*This poster of the divine
family depicts Shiva with
the* tripundraka *on his
brow and Ganesha
with an* Om *sign
on his hand.*

linga (see pp.66–7) and the "womb" of
nature or the cosmic waters. In Sanskrit
these two coalesce to become the *O* of
Om, and this union is symbolized by
the third element, the *m*. The union of
the apparent opposites
of earthly existence, fire
and water, might be seen
as encapsulated in the
shape of the syllable as a
pictograph in which a
single, curved line
emerges from the dual
shape (the 3) of the
bipartite body of the
symbol. The fourth ele-
ment, represented by the
dot, or *bindu*, which is
placed above the pic-
tograph's crescent moon
(see left), stands for the

"absolute spirit"
of *brahman* that
inhabits the other
three elements.

The pictograph represents
the Hindu concept of the trinity, and of
the fourth element that transcends it.
The *Mandukya Upanishad* associates it
with the four states of consciousness –
waking, sleeping, dreaming and *turiya*
(which is the transcendental self beyond
the conscious mind).

The pictograph is often said to be a
manifestation of *brahman,* the self that
transcends and unites the *trimurti* (see
pp.48–9) or trinity of the gods Brahma,
Vishnu and Shiva. It is also a representation of time (past, present and future)
and its transcendence, and of three of
the great sacred Vedic scriptures: *Rig,
Sama* and *Yajur*.

Tantra

Erotic carvings from one of the 11th-century temples at Khajuraho in Uttar Pradesh. Sexual intercourse played an important part in Tantric rituals.

Hindu Tantra is a highly unorthodox form of yoga. It has been developed as a mystical but very detailed path to ecstatic release which harnesses the infinite energies of mind and body. It is a yoga of action, not abstract contemplation. Rather than deny themselves the fruits of worldly pleasures, Tantrikas (Tantric practitioners) strive to gain the fullest possible pleasure from them. The experience or realization of their enjoyment reaches such high levels that the energy unleashed can carry consciousness to the peak of enlightenment.

The word *tantra* means "extension" or "warp" of the mind; it refers to sixty-four *Tantras* (religious texts) composed between the 5th and 8th centuries AD. These cover a wide range of subjects, from astrology to history and theology, and most are presented as dialogues between Shiva, usually acting as the guru, or teacher, and Shakti, his consort and pupil.

The Tantra movement was at its peak by the 10th century AD. Temples were built throughout northern India to the sixty-four *yoginis* (Tantric goddesses); in a golden age of Indian art, Tantric masons sculpted the remarkable erotic friezes at Khajuraho and Konarak.

There were two major strands to Tantra: the Left-hand (*vama-marga*) and Right-hand (*dakshina-marga*) paths. While the Right-hand way was practised by Tantra's more conservative followers, who concentrated on interpreting the texts intellectually, the Left-hand path was marked by esoteric ritual and body magic, especially the use of sexual intercourse.

Tantrikas generally rejected the notion of a remote, transcendent deity, knowable only through contemplation. Instead they honoured the *shakti* (manifest power) of godhead, incarnate in the form of Shakti, the goddess. This led them to believe that women were the "holders" of divine power. The union of male and female, transcendent and immanent godhead, was symbolized by ritual sexual intercourse.

Tantra associated physical sexual energy with the drive for the resolution of opposites, and visualized the human body itself as a plant whose roots feed on the pure energy of undiluted godhead. Like the sap of a plant, this energy was thought to flow through a network of veins that Tantrikas believed to be the "subtle body" formed about the axis of the spinal column (*sushumna*) (see also pp.94–5).

In this wood carving, from the Pashupati temple near Kathmandu, a scene of sexual union takes place before a demonic figure.

TANTRIC INITIATION

The guru's role in the Tantrika's quest for self-realization was so central that Tantra has often been defined as an initiation ritual in which a novice receives a personal *mantra* from his guru (see pp.98–9). Several Tantric gurus were women skilled in the sexual and yogic arts, and many of the Tantric saints were ritually initiated into their sects during sexual intercourse with a female "power holder". Sexual intercourse was believed to replicate the process of creation, whereby the "red energy" of the *yoni* (vulva), is continuously fertilized by the "white energy" of the seed.

Illustrations of sexual acts from a palm-leaf book of Tantric instructions produced in Orissa in the 19th century.

Festivals and pilgrimage

This modern poster depicts the Devi shrine at Paragadh, a popular place of pilgrimage in Maharashara.

With its wealth of religions, gods, goddesses, saints, heroes and saviours, it is not surprising that there is a religious festival in India on almost every day of the year. Some festivals are observed throughout the subcontinent, but most celebrate local deities and cults and mark the occasion of a god's incarnation, victory over a demon or marriage to a deity.

Holi is one of the most famous of India's festivals. It occurs on the day after the first full moon in March, when it can seem as if the entire population has congregated to celebrate the end of winter. Participants drink *bhang* (marijuana mixed with hot milk) and run through the streets, squirting ink and water and covering each other with brightly coloured powder (*galal*).

Every Hindu temple in India has a festival day. On this occasion, the statue of the residing deity is often taken out of the temple's inner sanctuary to be paraded through the streets and worshipped by its devotees. Male deities are often placed on thrones next to their consorts where they are entertained with singing, dancing and hymns of praise. Sacrificial blood may be offered to goddesses such as Kali, Durga (see pp.80–81) and Amman (see pp.106–7), whose worshippers offer their own bodies hoping to be ecstatically possessed.

The most sacred sites in India are known as *tirthas* (fords, see pp.166–7) between this world of ordinary experience and the divine realm of *brahman* (the godhead). They are often places of natural beauty, manifesting the power of the gods, and are usually found far from human dwellings – in the depths of forests, at the tops of mountains or in the most inaccessible caves.

The sites themselves, whether they be temples, rivers, or natural *lingas* (see pp.66–7), are believed to possess sacred power (*shakti*) which may be absorbed by the visiting devotee. Many pilgrims set out on a tour of specific sites.

ABOVE *A line of pilgrims make their way to the source of the Godavani river.*

LEFT *Devotees climbing up to the ice* linga *shrine at Amarnath in Kashmir.*

Buddhists may travel round the Ganges basin, where the historical Buddha lived, visiting the places associated with his life and death. Shiva worshippers may travel to the Himalayan settings of much Shaivite myth, or tour the sacred *jyotirlinga* sites, the twelve manifestations of Shiva's divine power. Vaishnavites, particularly those who worship Krishna, may make the round of areas associated with this god in the Mathura region. (See also pp.161–7 for a discussion of pilgrimage tours.)

SHIVARATRI

Shivaratri, one of India's biggest festivals, honours the power of the Shiva *linga*. Long ago a hunter killed too many animals and birds to carry them all home before dark, so he spent the night terrified and hungry up a tree. It was the night when there was no moon in the month of Phalgun (February / March) – a sacred night to Shiva. The hunter's constant trembling caused petals and dew to fall from the tree on to a *linga* beneath, and the god was pleased. When the hunter returned home and died on the following day, Shiva decreed that, since the man had worshipped the *linga* on the night of Shivaratri, he was fit to spend his afterlife on Mount Kailasa.

HOLI

One story associated with the Holi festival tells of an arrogant king who demands that all his subjects worship him. When the king's son refuses to comply, the king orders him to be put to death. The king's sister, Holika, goes with the prince to his execution and sits with him in the flames. Through her devotion the boy emerges unscathed, but Holika dies. Huge bonfires are now lit every year on the eve of the Holi festival to commemorate her death.

Holi is a boisterous festival in which participants are splattered with brightly coloured powder.

Rasa

Rasa is the Sanskrit word for the sap or juice of plants, but it has also long been used to describe the aesthetic pleasure which can be derived from works of art. *Rasa* can be felt when appreciating any of the arts; it can describe the rapt attention of an audience listening to a piece of music or of a spectator admiring a sculpture, or the mood evoked by looking at a painting. The 14th-century aesthetic theorist Vishvanatha uses the word *rasa* to help define the essence of poetry: "Poetry is a sentence, the soul of which is *rasa.*". Similarly, a lover may talk of *rasa* when describing the "essence of love".

Literally, *rasa* means liquid, juice or sap. The *rasa* of a pine tree is its resin, and lime juice is the *rasa* of a lime. It

Battle scenes such as this 17th-century miniature of a struggle between Rustam and the White Demon express raudra *(the furious) rasa.*

also signifies the essence of an object, not unlike the alchemical "quintessence", the mystical spiritual element which bound the four substantial elements of which an object was composed. By extension, *rasa* can mean taste or flavour, and is also used to describe the "feel" or atmosphere of a situation. On a higher level, *rasa* has come to signify the transcendent delight or bliss that unites artist and audience in a particular heightened mood. The closer the rapport, the more intense the *rasa*, and the more moving the mood of the work.

The *rasa* theory of Indian art was first expounded in the *Natyashastra*, written by the sage Bharata early in the 1st millennium AD. Bharata described various concomitant emotions, which awaken a particular *rasa* (flavour or feeling) in the *rasika* (viewer). He identified eight *rasas*, to which a ninth was added later: *shringara* (the erotic), *hasya* (the comic), *karuna* (the pathetic), *raudra* (the furious), *rira* (the heroic), *bhayanaka* (the terrible), *bibhatsa* (the odious), *adbhuta* (the marvellous) and *shanta* (the quiescent).

The *bhava* (mood or emotional state) of each *rasa* emerges from the combination of its *vibhavas* (determinants), *anubhavas* (consequents), and *vyabhicharibhavas* (complementary moods). The *bhava* of the *vira rasa*, for example, is *utsaha* (energy). The determinants of this heroic *rasa* are that there should be spirits or humans to conquer those who

The shringara *(erotic)* rasa *is illustrated in this 17th-century painting of Krishna dallying with Radha. Radha was Krishna's favourite among the* gopis *(see p.63).*

SHRINGARA RASA

Indian artists and critics are almost unanimous in acknowledging *shringara* (the erotic) as pre-eminent among the *rasas*. *Shringa* means peak, and the term *shringara* signifies the way in which the peak, or ecstasy, is reached. Much *shringara* art and sculpture is remarkably overt in its eroticism. Miniatures that were painted in Rajasthan during the 17th, 18th and 19th centuries frequently depict the passion that the divine Krishna felt felt for the *gopi* Radha (see p.63), while the figures that adorn the temples of Konarak and Khajuraho are among the most famous erotic sculptures in the world (see pp.110–11). Passion is also conveyed in a more subtle manner, in keeping with the *bhava* (mood) of *shringara*, which is *rati* (love), both human and divine. The *rasa* can be conveyed by its *vibhavas* (determinants), such as a moonlit garden, or by *anubhavas* (consequents), which may include a bashful, yearning glance.

deserve defeat in battle. The *anubhavas* (consequences) of the *vira rasa* are the seeking of allies and self-sacrifice, while the *vyabhicharibhavas* (complementary moods) are pride, valour and resolve. A knowledgeable audience would recognize each of these conditioning factors in the performance or presentation of a work of art.

COLOURS AND GODS

Each *rasa* is represented by a colour and a presiding deity. Shiva is the presiding deity of *hasya*, the comic *rasa*, for example, which is represented by the colour white. To see a reference to the storm god Rudra in a painting, indicates that the artist is conveying the *raudra* (furious) *rasa*, with its attendant *krodha* (mood of anger).

Village art

Embroidery is an exclusively female occupation in India and women from extended families often work together on designs. The pattern and stitchwork on such pieces are handed down from generation to generation. In some areas of the country, such as Gujurat, villages that are often only a short distance apart have their own highly distinctive patterns and colours.

The explorer Marco Polo said of rural India in the 13th century: "embroidery is here produced with more delicacy than anywhere in the world". In the villages, where nearly three-quarters of the Indian population still lives, embroidery as well as other arts continue to flourish. Village temples are adorned with a profusion of sculpted images and icons; small workshops turn out embroidery, carpets, silks, textiles and printed cloth to meet an ever-growing demand. Every region has its own unique artistic skill and is renowned for the use of particular materials.

Herbal paste is used to make auspicious marks on a bride's hands prior to marriage.

Village art is not confined to the workshop. In southern India, householders decorate their doorsteps with intricate patterns known as *kolamas* which are drawn in powder. The steps are wiped clean at night so that a new pattern can be created in the morning. *Kolamas* are often placed within a circle and, like *mandalas* (see pp.100–101), they are representations of the cosmos. In Tamil Nadu in southern India, they are known as "forts", "containers of sacred space".

The patterns of *kolamas* are usually based upon the hexagon, the

Women are responsible for maintaining and decorating their homes, and for refurbishing the ochre and whitewash on mud walls, as in this village in Rajasthan.

HOMEMADE GODS

There is a strong tradition in rural India of creating images only to destroy them again, returning them to the earth, or "womb", from which they came. Gods are depicted in highly abstract forms. They are often crudely fashioned from mud, and may even be represented by a simple ball of clay. Pillaiyar, the child-Ganesha, is the deity most often worshipped in this way. A piece of mud is moulded into a rough likeness of an elephant's head. When "eyes" made of silver foil or white stones are added, the image is said to assume the god's power (*shakti*). Villagers worship the image of Pillaiyar by placing flowers, coconuts (representing the three eyes of Shiva), and sweets around it. When the worship is over, they either

In a Bhil community in Rajasthan, coloured foil adorns household images.

throw the image in water or leave it to disintegrate into the soil. In Karnataka an image of Mariamman, the goddess of smallpox, was passed from village to village before being immersed in a river, carrying away with it the villages' disease.

overlapping triangles known in India as "the star of Lakshmi". They sometimes depict intertwined serpents, tortoises and crows – animals often at the centre of local folklore. *Kolamas* are drawn to protect the household against the spirits of the dead. The patterns made in henna on young girls' hands serve a similar symbolic purpose. Like *kolamas*, these patterns often lead toward a central dot (*bindu*) or focal point that attracts and distracts the "evil eye", absorbing its destructive power in the lines of the design.

Preparation of a kolama, an intricate pattern in white or coloured powder, on the mud threshold is a typical early morning task for the women of this household.

Music

Sound (*nada*) is believed to be at the heart of the process of creation. In Hindu myth, the sacred syllable *Om* (see pp.108–10) embodies the essence of the universe – it is the "hum" of the atoms and the music of the spheres – and sound in general represents the primal energy that holds the material world together.

The principles of Indian music are traditionally believed to be already present in the verses and recitation of the *Samaveda* (see pp.16–17), a collection of *samans* (chants) sung by the *udgatri* priests who officiated at the *soma* sacrifice. Because of their inclusion in the Vedic texts, musical scales, aesthetics, basic rhythms and systems of musical notation are all considered to be sacred. Therefore, the basic principles which govern rhythm, harmony and *raga* (melodic mood) are broadly common throughout the regional traditions of Indian classical music.

A *raga* is a particular melodic "framework" or underlying potential structure, somewhere between "tune", "scale" and "mode". The numerous different *ragas* are considered to be based on scales consisting of *svaras* – musical pitches or notes. Singing is traditionally viewed as the purest form of

Brass-players at the Pushkar fair in Rajasthan.
INSET *A* bahina *drum.*

A statue of a female drummer from the 13th-century temple at Konarak.

music, but a musician may also be acclaimed if the audience judges that his or her instrument is perfectly attuned to the human voice, so that the instrument and the singer are in complete harmony.

Each *raga* is suffused with a specific mood (*bhava*) and flavour (*rasa*), and may only be sung at certain times of the year, or at specific moments during the day or night. In early treatises, the *svaras* of each *raga* are sometimes also associated with colours, animals and attendant deities.

The *tala* is the music's basic metrical structure. A composition and its performance, which will often be extended by structured improvisation, will have a particular *tala,* and the drummer may only improvise between its constituent main beats. Unlike common practice in

Western music, the beats within the *tala* are not necessarily grouped in identical subunits, but may occur in asymmetrical groups. In any case, each such group is functionally different. There are many different *talas*, all of which can be played at a fast, medium or slow tempo.

There are two main traditions of classical music – the Hindustani school of northern India and the Karnatak school of the south. The principles and rules governing each branch are broadly the same, but regional variations employ different series of *ragas* and different methods in their elaboration. The Karnatak school adheres quite strictly to traditional and indigenous rules and precepts, unlike the Hindustani school which is more strongly influenced by Persian and Central Asian cultures. The Karnatak *ragas* bear mostly Sanskrit names and conform to sacred rules and structures, whereas in the Hindustani tradition, they carry the names of the dialects and regions from which they emerged, and are characterized by regional patterns of improvisation.

TEMPLE INSTRUMENTS

Music plays an important role in daily worship in the temples of southern India. A typical village temple will have three musicians: one playing a long brass horn (*nagasvaram*) and the other two playing drums such as the *tavil.* The *nagasvaram* horn is a melody instrument and uses the full range of notes – *sa, ri, ga, ma, pa, dha* and *ni*. Sounds made by the percussion instruments are known by a system of spoken syllables. The drums and the horn are heard whenever the temple's gates are opened or closed, and when a deity is presented to the villagers. Their music is matched to a phonetic structure, forming a language that is "spoken" between the instruments.

The dahina, one of the pair of drums in the tabla.

THE SITAR

The *sitar* is the dominant solo instrument in Hindustani classical music, and is usually accompanied by the *tambura* (drone lute) and *tabla* (drums). It is a member of the lute family, and is strongly influenced by the Persian long-necked lute – the *tabor*. The *sitar* has five melody strings, five or six drone strings (which also accentuate the base rhythm) and from nine to thirteen

"sympathetic" strings, all strung across a pear-shaped wooden body.

One of the most successful people in stimulating Western appreciation of Indian music is the musician and composer Ravi Shankar. Born in Varanasi, he began his career as a dancer, but then decided to concentrate on the *sitar*. He has made extensive tours of Europe and the United States, and in 1967 founded the Kinnara School of Music in Los Angeles.

LEFT *Ravi Shankar playing the* sitar.

BELOW *Wedding musicians at Kolhapur in Maharashtra.*

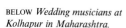

Dance

Like most of the arts in India, the principles of dance have their origins in the *Vedas* (see pp.16–17). A treatise on dramaturgy written in the early centuries AD relates a rebellion of the gods against the control of ritual and worship held by the *brahmin* priests. The gods appealed to Brahma to reveal a new *Veda*, detailing forms of dance and drama by which they could be worshipped by anyone, irrespective of their order. Thus the *Natya Shastra*, the fifth *Veda*, was revealed to the sage Bharata.

Dance is therefore a ritual, a symbolic form of worship performed at almost every ceremony in social and religious life. Dancers are hired for civic functions, weddings, births, harvests and religious processions. Dance is sacred, and dancers are "auspicious" because, like *brahmins,* they bring the blessings of the gods. The cultural diversity of India is reflected in the many folk dances and local variations on the five main styles of classical dance: *bharata-natyam*; *kathakali*; *kathak* (an upright, rhythmic style from northern India); *orissi* (a sinuous style similar to *bharata-natyam*, which is only performed by women) and *manipuri* (a less technically demanding

An 18th-century painting of a courtly dancer from Rajastan.

style from Manipur). Each of these styles is based to a varying extent on the principles in the *Natya Shastra*, which are passed down through the generations by gurus.

The best known solo style is *bharata-natyam*, the celebrated, classical dance of Tamil Nadu and Karnataka, which closely follows the *Natya Shastra*. The "pure dance" is *nritta*; an abstract expression of ecstasy in the technique of dancing. By contrast, *nritya* is dance in the service of drama, and uses *sahityas* (verses), *hastas* (hand gestures) and *abhinayas* (facial expressions), which signify phrases or ideas. Initially *bharata-natyam* was danced within temple walls by *devadasis* (servants of god), young female dancers who were symbolically married to the temple god. Gradually the dance moved out of the temples and into the courts. The *devadasis* became *ranjanadasis* (slaves for entertainment) and, during British colonial rule, *bharata-natyam* was little more than a form of soliciting. Victorian social reformers tried to ban the dance, and it was only revived,

This performer in Andhra Pradesh enacts the role of a tiger devil in a trance-inducing dance.

KATHAKALI

Kathakali, the sacred dance of Kerala in southern India, is among the most elaborate and sophisticated of the country's dance-dramas. The highly decorated characters depict gods and demons of the *Puranas* and the *Mahabharata,* enacting episodes from the great war between the forces of good and evil. Traditionally an all-night temple dance, *kathakali* produces a sense of harmony and well-being in performers and audience alike. The all-male dancers are adorned with billowing skirts, elaborate headdresses and ornate make-up. They stand relatively still upon the stage, telling their story with intricate hand gestures and eye movements that act as "words" in their symbolic dialogue. Their clothes and make-up also act as symbols. Green stands for mobility, a pattern of green and red for anger, black for demons and hunters, and orange for women and *brahmins.*

Costume and colour play a vital part in the complex symbolic language of kathakali. *Pith balls on the ends of actors' noses and fronts of their crowns represent nobility and differences of symbolic ranks.*

and performed in public, in the 1930s, in the wake of a growing Western fascination with the fake orientalism of dancers such as Ram Gopal.

Much of the content of classical dance is drawn from Hindu mythology and local legend. The great epics such as the *Mahabharata* (see pp.56–7) are sources of characters and themes for many dances, and the lives of the *avatars* such as Krishna and Rama inspire many of their *bhavas* (moods).

Several of these are strongly influenced by the *bhakti* (devotional) movement in southern India, which made human love a metaphor for a love of the divine, and the *nayaka-nayika* (hero-heroine) *bhava* is one of the most enduring themes of Hindu dance. The famous story in Hindu myth of Krishna's love for Radha and the *gopis* (see p.63) is often presented as a dance in which each of the *gopis* believes the man-god to be her partner.

Time and the Universe

In India science and religion are not opposed
fundamentally, as they often seem to be in
the West, but are seen as parts of the same
great search for truth and enlightenment that
inspired the sages of Hinduism, Buddhism
and Jainism. Thus, in the Hindu scientific
approach, understanding of external reality
depends on also understanding the godhead.

In all Hindu traditions the universe is said
to precede not only humanity but also the
gods. The Buddhists and Jains do not even
recognize a creator; for them time has no
beginning and no end. Jain cosmology and
metaphysics are particularly elaborate, being
at times sufficiently detailed to recognize
"atoms" *(pudgala)* as one of the five basic
entities permeating the universe.

Fundamental to Hindu concepts of time
and space is the notion that the external
world is a product of the creative play of
maya (illusion, see pp.130–31). Accordingly,
the world as we know it is not solid and real
but illusory. The universe is in constant flux
with many levels of reality; the task of the
saint is to find release (*moksha*) from the
bonds of time and space.

*Varanasi (right), India's most sacred city, is said to be outside
the usual restrictions of time and space. Pilgrims come from all
over the subcontinent to the "eternal city" to bathe in the holy
river Ganges, where they hope to wash away negative karma
acquired in the past. Varanasi has been a major centre of Indian
philosophy, religion and science since the 1st millennium BC.*

The soul

The *mantra, "Tat Tvam Asi"* ("Thou art That"), is the central dictum of the *Upanishads* (see pp.22–3). It defines the relationship between Thou, the *atman* (soul in every being), and That, the transcendent *brahman* (Absolute), which pervades the whole universe.

Brahman cannot be comprehended by the human mind; it is impersonal, infinite and immovable, beyond any definition. Although it is ineffable, there is a spark of *brahman* in every being, animating it with *atman.* We cannot grasp *brahman*, for it is not a distinct entity, but it might be visualized as sunlight upon the surface of a lake.

The *atman* is invariably described in negative terms, as it cannot be defined positively: it is intangible and indestructible, it cannot suffer nor can it die, for it is immortal in a mortal body. Yet although the *atman* is beyond human reason, the *Upanishads* taught that it is attainable by means of meditation, asceticism and yoga. No longer could the *brahmin* priests claim sole access to the Vedic gods and so to divinity, for the gods themselves could now be transcended by mystical experience. Rather than sacrifice, the main focus and goal of Hinduism was now *moksha* (release) – the ultimate freedom that comes with

These two pujaris (priests) are bathing at twilight in the sacred Narmada River, Madhya Pradesh. Washing in holy water cleanses the soul and removes the bad effects of past karma.

the knowledge that *brahman* and *atman* are finally one and the same.

The 8th-century AD theologian Shankara gave perhaps the clearest exposition of these *advaita* (non-dualist) views. He stressed the distinction between the realm of *brahman* and the world of ordinary experience, in which our individual egos believe themselves to have separate identities. For Shankara, liberation was not only the realization of our identity with the Absolute, but also our recognition of the illusory nature of the world, which is produced by the illusions of *maya* (see pp.130–31). Shankara argued that

reality exists at two distinct levels: ordinary and higher truth. At the ordinary level, the material world of objects and separate egos *is* real, but at the higher level it is illusory. The aim of the ascetic meditator, said Shankara, is to transcend the illusion of ordinary reality by uniting the Absolute with the soul.

Shankara's belief that there are no individual souls and that the Absolute is attainable through meditation, led to accusations that he was a crypto-Buddhist. In fact, he often attacked Buddhist doctrines, but there are similarities in the approaches of the two schools. The Buddha asserted not only that there is no separate soul, but that there is no soul at all: the doctrine of *anatta* (non-soul). The Buddha taught that suffering (*dukkha*) is caused by misguided identification with the individual self or ego, which is not eternal but temporary. The "I" that we imagine throughout life, is, according to the Buddha, both illusory and dispensable.

The Noble Eightfold Path (see p.35) was the Buddha's method of transcending the illusion of isolated selfhood by undoing the mental habits that keep the mind attached to a false idea of the self. From birth the concept of the self is protected and cultivated. The Buddha taught that the self which motivates our actions is the product of wrong desires. The self, the Buddha argued, does not exist, it cannot be found in the body, nor can it be defined; it is merely a word that is used to describe a temporary state.

The nature of death

Death is often likened to a night's sleep before rebirth. Just as we are the same person when we awake in the morning despite our consciousness having been absent for the night, so the *atman* (soul) passes smoothly from one body to another while consciousness sleeps. Only the body dies, which is a temporary shell whose components return to their sources when burnt by cremation – the "eye to the sun" and the "breath to the wind". The Hindu funeral liturgy does not talk of the past deeds of the dead person, but speaks directly to the soul – "depart, depart by the ancient paths of our ancestors" – for the soul is indestructible and will never die.

One of the most famous Vedic accounts of the cause of death is in the *Katha Upanishad*. A young *brahmin* man is sent to the Otherworld by an irritable father. He is the first human to visit the realm of Yama, the Lord of Death. Yama is busy and at first he ignores the *brahmin*. To atone for this initial discourtesy Yama offers the mortal three boons.

A statue of the king of death on the roof of the Korisha monastery.

For his third boon the *brahmin* asks to know the secret of death. Yama replies that death is an illusion caused by ignorance of the immortality of the soul which, according to the *Bhagavad Gita* (see pp.60–61), "is not slain when the body is slain". Yama concludes that the only way to escape death is to conquer it by transcending the individual self.

At the time of initiation, many *sadhus* (see pp.70–71) ritually act out their own deaths to represent the death of the individual self and the transcendence of the ego. However, these doctrines of the soul are not easy to understand and demand great emotional fortitude. In India there are many groups who to not believe in reincarnation, but say instead that the dead pass on to another realm, often in the Underworld.

Regardless of belief about the afterlife, attachment to one's former life can be a major problem. Shady groves on the outskirts of a village may be the haunts of the dangerous ghosts (*preta*) of suicides, women who die in childbirth, and misers who died without revealing the whereabouts of their hoard. Belief that those unable to

Funeral pyres at the edge of the sacred river Ganges in Varanasi, considered by Hindus to be the most auspicious place to be cremated.

accept their death cannot move on, suggests there is some idea of a personal identity, which survives death.

The traditional Hindu funeral method is cremation, the fire being seen as the means of conveying the soul to the next life. The sacred city of Varanasi is the most auspicious place to die; Hindus travel from all over India to be cremated there and to have their ashes scattered in the Ganges. The rituals that surround death are highly significant. At a *shraddha* funeral, for example, food is offered to *brahmin* priests for the benefit of the deceased. This rite is re-performed at least once a year to ensure the positive rebirth of the dead relative.

JAIN DEATH

Sallekhana is the Jain religious death of wasting away through controlled fasting. Jains share with Hindus and Buddhists the belief that correct action at the moment of death can directly influence the next birth. In keeping with their belief that the practice of austerity and asceticism can affect rebirth (*samsara*) by the burning away of *karma* (see pp.44–5), the ideal Jain death is one in which the mind is in total control of the body. Fasting "scours out" the body of its negative *karma*, and the mind is thereby free at the moment of death to concentrate on its spiritual destiny. One of the most famous Jain accounts of *sallekhana* concerns Skhandala, a disciple of Mahavira, who abandoned food, drink and care of his body until, after rejecting sixty meals, he died deep in meditation.

SATI

A widow who has immolated herself on the funeral pyre or grave of her dead husband is known as a *sati* (suttee). The word *sati* shares its root with the Sanskrit *satya* (virtuous way or truth) and thus means a woman who has followed the right and virtuous path. The truest woman in Hindu mythology was Sati, Shiva's first consort (see p.74), in whose name widows sacrifice themselves for their husbands.

Self-immolation was widely practised in India before it was made illegal in 1829 and handprints, such as those on the wall in Jodhpur Fort, mark the spot where *satis* died after their husbands fell in battle. The British found it one of the hardest Indian customs to understand and sympathize with. In early 19th-century Calcutta there was an upsurge of widow-burnings, which may have been in response to the enormous cultural changes introduced by British rule. Since then there have been sporadic revivals of *sati* up to the present day.

This painting of a sati demonstrates the honour in which such action was held.

Handprints of women who immolated themselves at Jodhpur Fort.

Concepts of time

The transcendence of time is the aim of every Indian spiritual tradition. Time is frequently presented as the enemy, as an eternal wheel that binds the soul to a mortal existence of ignorance and suffering. "Release" from time's fateful wheel is termed *moksha*, and an advanced ascetic may be called *kala-atita* ("he who has transcended time").

The *Atharvaveda* (see pp.16–17) suggested that time was "the first principle", by which the universe was created and put into motion. It is, however, more common to read in Hindu texts of attempts to "cheat" or "vanquish" time. A verse from the *Mahabharata* (see pp.56–7) advises that "time 'cooks' all beings" and "destroys all creatures"; when everything else sleeps "time is awake, time is hard to overcome".

Time in Hindu mythology is conceived of as a wheel turning through vast cycles of creation (*sarga*) and destruction (*pralaya*), known as *kalpa*. Classical Hindu texts understand each *kalpa* to be a life of the creator god Brahma. He is said to live for 100 Brahmic years, which are equivalent to 311,040,000,000,000 human years. The universe appears at his birth and is destroyed at his death. A new Brahma is born after a further 100 Brahmic years and the cycle begins again. Each *kalpa* is made up of 1,000 "great aeons", which in turn are composed of four *yugas* (world ages). Each cycle of *yugas* sees a gradual deterioration of

A chariot wheel of the sun god, Surya, from the temple at Konarak in Orissa.

morality, awareness and well-being. The present age (Kali Yuga) is the last in the cycle and marks the point at which spiritual intelligence and morality have reached their lowest ebb.

The Jains see time as a wheel with six ascending and six descending "spokes" or eras. The wheel revolves for eternity – it was never born nor will it ever end. In Buddhism, time is the "devourer", the enemy of all living beings. The main reason why existence (*bhava*) is full of suffering (*dukkha*) is because of the passage of time, and a process somewhat like the idea of entropy. The Buddha's last words were said to begin, "All things decay…".

In the *Yoga Sutra*, time is conceived as a discontinuous series of "moments" (*kshanas*). Each "moment" represents the amount of time that it takes for an atom (*anu*) to shift from one position to another. Unlike the passage of time these "moments" are said to be real.

THE FOUR YUGAS

The first world age is Satya Yuga – the golden age of innocence and truth which is slowly tarnished until the arrival of the Treta Yuga, and the gradual decrease of virtue and length of life. Next is the Dvapara Yuga, in which the heroes of the *Ramayana* and *Mahabharata*, such as Krishna and Rama, are said to have lived. The world age in which we now live is Kali Yuga (the name is not related to the goddess Kali). This age is characterized by vice, violence, ignorance and greed.

TANTRIC TIME

Tantra depicts time as a ladder which descends in clear stages of devolution from the original unity which preceded creation to the present world of differentiation and illusion. With the steps marked out in sacred texts, Tantrikas sought to "turn around" (*paravritti*) and climb back up the ladder. In doing so they would be reversing the usual process of time.

Whereas both Christian theology and Western physics understand the origins of the universe to be a definable point far back in linear time that is now lost to us, Tantric science sees the creation as a continuous process, and one therefore that is always available to our understanding.

A common Tantric symbol depicts the past as being constantly projected from the present, like a flow of events being vomited from the open mouth of a monster. It is not that things began at some distant point in the past, but that the past is continually projected from and through the present space-time "mouth" of our own consciousnesses.

Since Tantra equates the inner consciousness with the higher consciousness that permeates the universe, Tantrikas believe that they can "turn around" the outer cosmic process of creation and devolution by "looking back" into the monster's mouth within. Therefore, through the process of meditation, Tantrikas can absorb themselves in the continuous act of creation that works through our individual and collective consciousnesses.

THE SERPENT OF INFINITY

According to Hindu belief, the universe is destroyed at the end of each *kalpa* (life of the creator god, Brahma). Between the destruction of the world and its re-creation, at the end of each cycle, Vishnu is said to rest in the coils of Ananta, the great serpent of infinity, while he waits for the universe to re-create itself. At the end of Kali Yuga, the present age, it is believed that Vishnu will descend in the form of his tenth and final *avatar* – as Kalki, the warrior, riding upon a white horse. He will destroy ignorance, drive invaders from India, and save the good, from whom the people of the golden age, the Satya Yuga, will descend.

Vishnu asleep on the coils of the serpent Ananta, emblem of the timeless cosmos, in a polychrome relief on the temple at Srirangam, Tamil Nadu.

Maya

In much of Hindu thought *maya* is illusion, and what humankind understands to be reality is in fact the dream of Brahma (see pp.48–9). He is the creator god and great magician who dreams the universe into being. The dream itself is maintained by Vishnu, the Preserver, who uses *maya* to spin the complex web that we know as reality. It is not that the world itself is an illusion, only our perception of it. Whereas we suppose the universe to be made up of a multitude of objects, structures and events, the theory of *maya* asserts that all things are one. Rational categories are mere fabrications of the human mind and have no ultimate reality.

Rajneesh, one of the most famous of the modern Indian spiritual teachers (see pp.154–5), asserted that if the West had followed the Greek philosopher Heraclitus rather than Plato, the history of ideas would be very different and the concept of *maya* would be central to Western as well as to Eastern thought. Although Plato's teaching resembles *maya* when he writes that "the visible world is a pale shadow of a true reality beyond", he believed that each aspect of the world had a separate, distinct identity. Heraclitus posited instead a theory which was based on the assumption of the inseparable interconnectedness of the universe. His Theory of Becoming asserts that all things are in a state of constant flux; always in the process of becoming something else. This hypothesis is echoed today, some 2,500 years later, by Chaos Theory, which the American science writer James Gleick defined as "the science of process rather than state, of becoming rather than being".

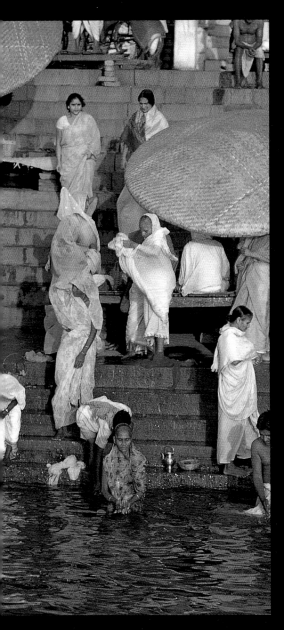

WATERS OF ILLUSION

The Greek philosopher Heraclitus used a river as an analogy for his Theory of Becoming, teaching that one cannot step into the same river twice. *Maya*, too, is often associated with water, the medium that forever changes as it flows from place to place. Water is both a symbol and an agent of illusion. When Vishnu is compelled to lift the veils of *maya* for the benefit of his followers, water is never far away. A well-known Hindu parable tells of a sage who underwent such rigorous penance that he felt entitled to demand from Vishnu the secret of *maya*. The god responded by ordering the mortal to dive into a nearby river. When the sage emerged, he did so as a woman, oblivious of her former existence. After a lifetime of success and failure, happiness and tragedy, she finally threw herself in despair onto the funeral pyre of her husband, who had been murdered. The fire was instantly quenched by water. The sage regained his former body, and in that moment Vishnu appeared. "This is *maya*," he said, and the sage came to understand the nature of illusion and the workings of the universe.

Pilgrims immersing themselves in the sacred waters of the Ganges river at Varanasi.

Creation

Vishnu sleeping on the cosmic ocean, as depicted on a carved boulder set in a pond outside Kathmandu.

In keeping with the importance of sacrifice in Aryan India, one of the best-known Vedic creation myths relates the sacrifice of *purusha,* the cosmic man. The gods cut up *purusha,* took the quarter of him that was manifest in their realm and placed it upon the sacrificial fire; from this the Vedic deities Indra, Agni and Vayu were born, together with the cardinal points of the universe, animals, humans and the four *varnas* (orders).

Other accounts in the *Vedas* speak of a cosmic egg or embryo from which "the lord of creation" was born as the great oceans heated up. But later hymns were increasingly sceptical of such symbolism; the tenth book of the *Rigveda* includes a verse asking: "Who truly knows, who could here declare whence was born, whence comes this creation?"

Whereas in Western religions a creator god precedes man and the universe,

the Hindu gods are preceded by creation; the origin of the world is envisaged not so much as an act of creation but as one of organization, the making of order out of chaos. The universe is often said to be born from the sacred syllable *Om* (see pp.108–9), or from an inert void in which "there was neither being nor non-being ... death nor non-death", a single principle from which emerged the diversity of life. From this void desire was born, and from desire came humans, gods and demons.

In the *Brhadaranyaka Upanishad's* version of creation the universe was pure Self in the form of a man, existing alone without a Creator. It looked around and saw nothing but itself, shouted "I am!" but then felt afraid, and, "lacking delight", divided itself into two parts for company. The half that was She asked, "How can he unite with me, who am produced from himself?", and she went to hide from him. She became a cow, but he turned into a bull and united with her; she became a mare, goat, sheep and ass, but each time he found her, and became himself a stallion, ram and buck, and the world was thus populated.

The half that was He then realized, "I am creation, for I have poured forth all this." It was not that man was born in a god's image, but that all of creation was born from the cosmic man. God and humankind are thus of the very same flesh, that of the first being who wanted to be more, and so divided. "Anyone understanding this," the hymn concludes, "becomes, truly, himself a creator in this creation."

This pair of 6th-century carved panels belongs to a rock-cut shrine at Badami in the state of Karnataka. Varaha (far left), the third incarnation of Vishnu, is characteristically shown here as a boar, while Vamana (left), the fifth incarnation of Vishnu, is depicted pacing out the dimensions of the universe.

CHURNING THE OCEAN

One version of this myth tells how, soon after the universe had been created, the gods (*devas*) set out to churn the great ocean of milk to obtain *soma*, the elixir of immortality. Promising them a share, they invited the demons (*asuras*) to take the tail of the serpent Vasuki, wrapped about the giant churning pole like a rope. The pole was fixed to the bottom of the ocean and the waves it made in twisting one way and the other threatened to destroy the three worlds. Vishnu incarnated himself as the tortoise Kurma, taking the pole on his back to prevent the commotion. Glorious treasures emerged from the churned milk, followed by the goddess Lakshmi. A terrible poison then came forth. Shiva himself swallowed it, however, and by yogic power kept it in his throat so it would not harm him.

An 18th-century painting of the churning of the ocean with Kurma and Vasuki.

Shiva Nataraja

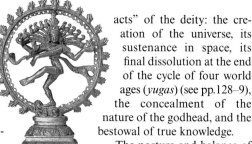

Throughout southern India, Shiva is worshipped as Shiva Nataraja, Lord of the Dance. In the words of Ananda Coomaraswamy, a pioneering Hindu philospher and historian of Indian art, Shiva's dance is the "clearest image of the activity of God which any art or religion can boast".

Shiva dances in a halo of flames symbolizing his radiating energy, as shown in a modern brass image.

Shiva's dance is a symbol of the unity and rhythm of existence. The unending, dynamic process of creation and destruction is expressed in the energetic posture of the god. Shiva dances in a ring of fire that refers to the life-death process of the universe. Everything is subject to continual change, as energy constantly assumes new forms in the "play" (*lila*) of creation, except the god himself whose dance is immutable and absolute. The pictorial allegory of Nataraja indicates the so-called "five acts" of the deity: the creation of the universe, its sustenance in space, its final dissolution at the end of the cycle of four world ages (*yugas*) (see pp.128–9), the concealment of the nature of the godhead, and the bestowal of true knowledge.

The posture and balance of Nataraja's dancing form show Shiva in the aspect of *tamas*, the expansive centrifugal force that creates and destroys the universe. This is the first of the three "tendencies" (*gunas*) that permeate the universe in Sankhya philosophy. *Tamas* (darkness), symbolized by Shiva, is responsible for the constant birth, change and death of all things; the force *sattva* (tranquillity), represented by Vishnu the Preserver (see pp.48–9), holds the atoms of every object together. These two "tendencies" – one holding the atoms of the universe

The temple at Chidambaram in southern India is believed to mark the actual site of the dance contest in which Shiva emerged triumphant.

CHIDAMBARAM

Chidambaram, the mythical site of Shiva's cosmic dance, has been the centre of Shaivite art and thought for over a millennium. Its great temple, built by successive southern Indian dynasties between the 10th and 16th centuries AD, is dedicated to Shiva Nataraja, and is said to be the site of his legendary dance in the presence of his consort Parvati (see pp.74–5). Shiva's dancing icon resides in the Golden Hall, a symbol of the nucleus of the atom and of the centre (*bindu*) of the universe. The *Upanishads*, *Vedas*, *Puranas* and other sacred Hindu texts are represented by parts of the temple complex, the temple as a whole standing for the totality of Hindu knowledge. Shiva's dance to Parvati is celebrated in a great festival in December.

This 19th-century painting from Tanjore, Tamil Nadu, shows Nataraja with Parvati inside the Golden Hall at Chidambaram, with the atoms whose dance he symbolizes.

together and the other ripping them apart – create a "friction" (*rajas*) that "vibrates" the world's atoms and creates the gravity to hold them to the earth. This is the third tendency, symbolized by the deity Brahma (see pp.48–9). It is the building stuff both of matter and of subtle energies such as perception and thought.

Consciousness inhabits all things and has permeated the universe since it was created from its original *bindu* (energy centre). The first stage of the universe was filled by "space": the potential area in which the world will "expand" with the energy of Shiva's aspect as *tamas*. At the end of Kali Yuga (the current age of ignorance), the "expansion" accelerates, everything merges and Shiva performs the terrible *tandava* dance of destruction.

EINSTEIN

There is a striking resemblance between the equivalence of mass and energy symbolized by Shiva's cosmic dance and the Western theory, first expounded by Einstein, which calculates the amount of energy contained in a subatomic particle by multiplying its mass by the square of the speed of light: $E = mc^2$.

Jain cosmology

The Jain universe (*loka*) is the most intricate cosmological system to have emerged from India. In Jain cosmology, time and space have neither beginning nor end. The world is infinite, impersonal and has no moral function: it was never created, it simply exists. The *loka* itself is a vast arena of fantastic dimensions in which an infinite number of souls are continually reborn.

Jain philosophy divides the universe into two categories: *jiva* (soul) and *ajiva* (non-soul). *Ajiva* comprises five basic entities, *dharma* (motion), *adharma* (rest), *pudgala* (atoms), *akasha* (space) and *kala* (time).

The *jiva* is said to be eternal, transcendent and made of "pure consciousness", motivated by an innate and absolute will. It is the *jiva* that experiences and perceives the world, through the eyes and ears of a body that is nothing more than an inert coagulation of atoms. The *jiva* controls every intellectual function of the brain, and is the sole recipient of spiritual knowledge and awareness. There are two types of embodied *jivas* – those that are motionless, including rocks and plants, and those capable of movement, including every insect, animal, god and human being. These forms of life are understood as being different, while also having inherent similarities, since all are *jivas* trapped in the inert matter of their bodily forms.

Of the many gods, demons, rocks, people and plants in whose forms the *jiva* is constantly reborn, only humans are capable of reaching *nirvana* in the course of their lives. This state of blessedness, in which the soul is freed from individuality and desires and released from the effects of *karma*, is, in Jain philosophy, the ultimate goal of human endeavour, and is achieved through many lifetimes of discipline and asceticism. The gods are assigned inferior positions in the cosmology, although some of them are worshipped by Jains to win wealth or protection; because they live in heaven, their merit from good *karma* is sure to be quickly used up and they will be plunged again into the piteous round, reborn as dust, a rock, a river, a cloud, bacteria, a newt, a hell-being and so on. Every phase of rebirth may last for up to 700,000 years, the outcome being dependent on the soul's own actions and *karma*.

The first Jain text to deal with the principles of time and space was the *Vyakhyaprajnapti* (*Exposition of Explanations*), initially compiled around the 3rd century BC and expanded later. This detailed what would finally become the customary shape for the *loka* – narrow in the middle with wider upper and lower sections. From the 16th century onward, the universe was widely depicted in the shape of a massive human form (*purusha*). This enormous entity has no will of its own, but is just a coagulation of non-soul matter held together by the delusion of the constantly transmigrating *jivas*.

The earth plane, where humans live, is represented as the middle level of the universe. Below are seven layers of hell, ending with the darkest, most cruel level at the universe's feet; above are fourteen increasingly celestial levels inhabited by different classes of gods. At the very top is the "slightly curving place", where liberated souls finally reside free from further rebirth.

MOUNT MERU

The world axis in Jain as in Hindu mythology is symbolized by Mount Meru – the mountain that is the centre of the universe, around which are rings of seven oceans, seven continents and the heavens. At its centre is the continent Jambudvipa, and to its south, flanked by the Himalayan mountains, is Bharata, the legendary India of old. All the major gods have heavenly kingdoms on or near it, and its roots reach down to the infernal regions.

The mosaic ceiling in the Kanch Mandir at Indore in Madhya Pradesh depicts the Jain universe; Mount Meru is represented in the middle.

TIME

Jain cosmology regards time as a twelve-spoked wheel, each cycle of which comprises two halves. The spokes represent world ages (*yugas*) which revolve eternally (see pp.128–9). Six of the spokes ascend (*utsarpini*) from darkness into light, and the other six descend (*avasarpini*) from a golden age into an age of violence, ignorance and confusion. The first age of the descending cycle is an era lasting many millions of years. In this most golden age, people are born 6 miles (10km) tall as perfect boy-girl twins that later marry and live in bliss, their every need satisfied by ever-bounteous wish-fulfilling trees. After three gradually degenerating world ages, sorrow enters the world and the Fordmakers (see pp.42–3) appear to offer release. This world age is known as *duhtcha* (sorrowful), the 21,000 year "uneven age". In the darkest world age at the bottom of the wheel of time, Jainism dies out and people live as dwarfs in shelters and caves. When it can get no worse, the ascending cycle begins, saviours appear to resurrect the Jain religion, and the golden age returns until it descends again, and the wheel of time continues to revolve for eternity.

Astrology

A 19th-century manuscript showing the eastern and western hemispheres of the heavens.

Astrology – throughout antiquity synonymous with astronomy – is known to have been practised in India for more than 1,500 years; its roots may be as old as that again. It was born from the merging of two great traditions – the *jyoti* science of divine astronomy outlined in the *Puranas* (see p.49), and the Western system of natal (birth) astrology developed by the ancient Greeks.

Indian and Western astrology have much in common, each recognizing the zodiac and the rule of the planets over the "signs". The earliest astrological texts in India were called the *Yavanajatakas* ("Greek birth astrology"), showing a typical absorption of foreign influence; but it was not long before *jyoti* elements began to re-emerge. The

resulting blend of Western and indigenous thought inspired a remarkable era of Indian astrology and science. The new astrologers had the benefit of both traditions and, realizing that the model of a flat earth could not account for the difference in the positions of the stars in India and ancient Greece, they evolved a new model, that of a spherical earth.

Perhaps the most important difference between modern Western and Indian astrology is that different systems are used to measure the passage of time. Where the West uses the "tropical" system to coordinate the zodiac with the actual rotations of the stars, India uses "sidereal" time. The sidereal system is based on the position of the stars in the sky, while the Western tropical model is a more abstract concept.

BRANCHES OF ASTROLOGY

Muhurta is "electional astrology", which divines the correct moment at which to begin an enterprise. *Vivaha* is "marriage astrology", which decides the eligibility of a couple and the most suitable time for marriage. It is common practice to advertise for marriage partners in India's newspapers, giving the astrological chart of the intended spouse.

Jaipur's observatory, used to view the Capricorn zodiac.

The steps at the Jantar Mantar (the 13th-century observatory at Delhi) are flanked by a calibrated scale for measuring the movement of the planets.

ASTRONOMY

The *jyotis* ("lights" or "heavenly bodies") were first studied in the *Vedangas*, a group of ancillary commentaries known as "the limbs of the *Vedas*", in c.400BC. Like the early astrology of the West, *jyoti* was considered a science, incorporating philosophy, astronomy and mathematics.

These first astronomers, or *jyotishas*, were largely concerned with establishing a religious calendar, based upon the movements of the moon as it passed through groups of twenty-seven or twenty-eight stars (known as "lunar mansions") in an apparent monthly cycle. Faced with the problem of the moon's irregularity from month to month, the *jyotishas* set out to discover a longer cycle, when it repeated itself exactly; this they found to be nineteen solar years.

The main function of the *jyotishas* – who were *brahmin* priests – was to use their knowledge of the stars to work out the most auspicious times for sacrifices to be held. Since the well-being of a kingdom was considered to be dependent upon the major sacrifices being carried out correctly, the role of the astrologer / astronomer was fundamental. An amendment to the *Atharvaveda* declared that "a king without an astrologer is like a boy without a father".

Hindu Temples

It was the resurgence of Hinduism in India from the 5th century AD onward that initiated a major stage in the development of religious art and architecture. Hindu temples had previously been built from wood, but imitating the examples of excavated Buddhist sanctuaries (see pp.36–7), Hindu architects began carving them from solid rock, affirming symbolic links with mountains and caves, the traditional homes of the gods.

Rock-cut temples mark a high point in technical skill and architectural imagination. Probably the most spectacular "mountain temple" in India is the so-called Kailasha at Ellora, in the modern state of Maharashtra. Carved out by the kings of the Rashtrakuta dynasty in the 8th and 9th centuries, the temple was created by removing gigan-

tic amounts of solid stone from the mountainside before completing the sculptural embellishments of the exterior and interior of the building.

At about the same time as the Kailasha was being created, structural techniques in architecture were being developed for temple projects. The Pallava kings who governed the Tamil country from the 7th to 9th centuries were important in these endeavours. Their capital, the ancient city of Kanchipuram, contained over one hundred Hindu shrines, each with a sanctuary distinguished by a pyramidal masonry tower. The achievements of the Pallavas were sustained in the 10th and 11th centuries by their successors, the Cholas, who were noted for erecting temples with great spires, as at Thanjavur, Gangaikond-acholapuram

---

THE ELLORA CAVE-TEMPLES

The term "cave-temple" fails to convey the magnificence and magnitude of the Ellora caves, situated near the village of Ellora in western India. The achievement of the Rashtrakuta architects may be compared to the carving of an entire cathedral out of solid rock.

There are thirty-two rock-cut temples in the Ellora complex. These are dedicated to the Hindu, Buddhist and Jain faiths and were built between the 6th and 9th centuries AD. The Kailasha temple, dedicated to Shiva and Parvati (see pp.74–5), is the centrepiece of the complex and stands 165 feet

(50m) long and 96 feet (29m) high. Free-standing "pillars of victory" are positioned around its central courtyard which houses galleries that are filled with icons and narrative reliefs.

This view of the courtyard of the Kailasha temple at Ellora demonstrates how the gallery and pillars have been cut from the rock-face. In the foreground stands a statue of an elephant.

THE TEMPLE AS MANDALA

Hindu temples are believed to be the earthly abodes of gods and goddesses. Each temple is built to uniform rules of sacred architecture and is devised to entice deities to take up residence. The building of temples was treated as a form of *puja* (worship), a ritual that provides access to divinity. Like a three-dimensional *mandala* (see pp.100–101), the temple was thought to be a microcosmic representation of the universe. At its centre is the icon of the deity, surrounded by images of his or her retinue, arranged in decreasing order of precedence to denote a divine hierarchy. Above the *sanctum sanctorum* (*garbhagriha*) in which the deity resides is the temple tower, representing Mount Meru, the mythical axis at the centre of the cosmos (see p.137).

Temple towers at Madurai (right) and Mamallapuram (below).

and Chidambaram. The central shrine at Thanjavur, major capital of the Cholas, is built entirely of granite, rising to a height of 207 feet (63m), making it the tallest shrine in southern India. The Thanjavur temple is celebrated for its stone and bronze sculpture, as well as for the narrative murals that cloak the interior walls of its dark passageways.

Subsequent dynasties refined original Chola models, adding more shrines and surrounding them with enclosure walls with impressive towered gateways known as *gopuras*. These massive structures stood twice as high as they were broad, looming not only over temple complexes but also over entire towns and their surrounding fields. The number of storeys on each *gopura* was generally uneven, the levels diminishing as they ascended until they reached the summit which was represented by a vaulted roof-form with arched ends.

In the 16th and 17th centuries, a renaissance of Hindu religion and culture in southern India under the kings of the Vijayanagara empire and their

A panorama of gods, goddesses, semi-divine beings and lesser figures populates the tower of the 18th-century Kapalishvara temple, Madras.

representatives once again led to a revival of temple building. Earlier religious institutions were renovated and expanded, giving rise to the invention of great temple cities with multiple shrines and rows of *gopuras* leading to the focal sanctuary. This building programme was partly due to the Hindu religion's affirmation of the temple as the central institution in sponsoring religious thought, literature and art.

Temples were not merely places where divinities were housed in order to receive worship from their devotees, they were in themselves representations of the heavenly realms. That the temple was conceived as a pantheon of gods and goddesses is evident from the carved and painted figures that covered their exteriors and interiors, and which comprised the most significant motifs in Hindu sacred art; this is particularly true of monuments in southern India. Large numbers of divinities populated the different tiers of the temple, ranging from the lowest levels where shrines were elevated on plinths, to the towers that soared over sanctuaries and entrance *gopuras*.

From the 16th century onward, the temple spires in southern India were covered with vivid, polychrome figures modelled in plaster. They depicted the major aspects and "family members" of

MAGICAL PROTECTION

Because of its sacred function as the home of the divine, the temple is vulnerable and needs to be shielded from unwanted negative forces, such as the Asura demons who wage a constant war against the *Devas* (gods). For this reason, doorways and openings are invariably guarded by armed figures. But protection extends beyond the mere show of weaponry. Auspicious river goddesses, recognized by aquatic monster – or tortoise – mounts, emblematic of the Ganges and Jumna, are a common sight. So too are amorous couples, their limbs entwined in a variety of intimate embraces. The sexual energy of these couples is identified with the forces of nature which ensure magical protection. Scenes with conjoined couples are found at the doorways of many Hindu shrines. In some temples, as at Khajuraho and Konarak, they form major compositions in their own right, signifying the magical protection required to guarantee the successful life of the temple.

Sexual energy is considered a strong magical force and is often represented on temple walls, such as this 11th-century temple at Khajuraho.

the deity to whom the sanctuary was dedicated, usually a form of Shiva, Vishnu or the mother goddess. But this sculptural profusion was by no means restricted to celestial personalities, since a whole range of lesser creatures also populated Hindu art. They ranged from aerial musicians, singers and dancers to fierce guardians clutching clubs and other weapons. Animals and birds also made an appearance, in particular those creatures which were the "vehicles" (*vahanas*) on which the gods and goddesses rode. Fantastic beasts with leonine heads and bodies, known in southern India as *yalis*, were ubiquitous. They decorated niches and arches, and were prominent motifs at the summits of temple towers.

The Mughals

The first and last great Mughal emperors of India, Babur and Aurangzeb, were poets. Although the first Islamic incursions into India were marked by violence and destruction, the Mughal emperors who ruled from 1526 to 1707 were generally tolerant of the indigenous religions. Their extravagance and power were reflected in the splendour of Mughal art and architecture.

The first Muslims to reach India were Arab merchants who arrived in the Punjab and the Sind in the 8th century AD to trade with local Hindu kings. From the 12th century, Turkish and then Afghan Sultans sent raiding parties into northern India on an almost annual basis. By 1340, the Sultanate of Delhi ruled twenty-four provinces, including parts of the Deccan and of the Malabar coast (in modern Tamil Nadu and Kerala). During the 15th century, the Hindu Vijayanagar and northern Rajput dynasties checked Islamic expansion in India, until the arrival of Babur, the first Mughal emperor, in 1526. Whereas the Delhi Sultanate have been seen as foreigners who plundered India for their own gain, the six great Mughal emperors are often said to have been Indians who happened to be Islamic. The Mughal period saw a gradual fusion of Hindu and Islamic thought, art and architecture. Akbar (1556–1605), who was perhaps the greatest emperor, took the daughter of a Hindu king as his wife, and the Mughals that succeeded him thus had Hindu as well as Islamic forebears. The Mughals employed Hindu generals, administrators, philosophers and artists in their courts. Their massive building programmes were only achieved by complete cooperation between the Mughals and local Hindu dynasties, and the most splendid mosques and mausoleums were built and carved by Hindu as well as Persian craftsmen. Whereas Hindu temples symbolized the outer universe with its multitude of gods, the Mughal mosques were built to symbolize Allah, the "one true god". Allah has many names but cannot be depicted. Instead of crowded images of personified divinities, Mughal mosques are light and airy and decorated with abstract geometric designs. As Islam teaches the ideas of burial and an afterlife (rather than Hindu cremation and rebirth) the emperors' tombs became a major form of Indian architecture. Huge mausoleums, such as the Taj Mahal and Akbar's tomb in Sikandra, are among India's finest buildings.

AKBAR'S TOLERANCE

Although it was Babur who founded the Mughal dynasty, Akbar is credited with being its greatest emperor. At the age of seventeen, he seized power from his advisers, and during the half century of his rule Akbar built an empire that was perhaps the most sophisticated culture and economy of its time in the world. Every official was paid a salary in coins, peasants were taxed according to their yield and, unlike their feudal counterparts in Europe, they had full rights of ownership over their land. Akbar did not attempt to subjugate but co-existed with the Hindu population of India. He wooed the Rajput kings by marrying the daughter of Raja Bharmal of Amber in 1562. In 1563 he abolished a tax that had been exacted from Hindu pilgrims on their way to sacred sites, and the following year he repealed the hated *jizya* poll tax paid by every non-Muslim.

The Taj Mahal was built on the southern bank of the Yamuna river, outside Agra, by Shah Jehan in memory of his beloved wife, Arjumand Banu Begam, also called Mumtaz Mahal ("Chosen One of the Palace"), from which the building got its name. The entire complex took over twenty years to build, employing more than 20,000 labourers.

Gurus

Since its central doctrines are fluid, Hinduism has not generally been a proselytizing religion dispatching missionaries around the world. It can be seen as the most tolerant and eclectic of the world's major religions. Rather than denying the existence of rival creeds, it embraces them, perceiving them as aspects of a single godhead whose many forms reflect the multiform nature of illusory reality.

   Yet the travelling Indian guru, arriving in foreign lands with a message of liberation and enlightenment, has recently become a familiar image of the spiritual East. The guru is an ambiguous figure to Western audiences. Gurus teach a path of self-denial, contemplation and the liberation of the soul from the grasp of matter, but they occasionally return to their homeland fabulously rich. Perhaps the most notorious was Bhagwan Rajneesh, the guru of the "orange people", who landed in the United States with the words, "I am the Messiah," only to leave in disgrace. Believing that everyone is essentially neurotic, Rajneesh attempted to break his devotees' attachment to their egos by shocking them out of their usual habits. Like Sai Baba, enlightenment came to Rajneesh at an early age, and he did not hesitate to proclaim his own divinity. Gandhi, by contrast, called himself a "humble seeker after truth", but millions have honoured him as a saint.

Among the miniature images of Shiva and Ganesha on sale in this village stall is an icon of Sai Baba of Shirdi and a photograph of Swami Muktananda, two of India's most popular 20th-century gurus. India's gurus are human beings, yet they take their place alongside the gods as objects of worship and reverence.

Guru Nanak

Although the Sikhs constitute only two per cent of India's population, they have had a disproportionately profound influence on the political and spiritual development of the subcontinent.

The principle which the founder, Guru Nanak, established as the basis of Sikhism is a belief in one, transcendent, inexpressible and formless divinity, who is manifest everywhere in the world he has created – a concept very similar to Hindu *brahman* (see p.48). Nanak used many names for this god, including the names of several Hindu gods and many of the Islamic names which are used to describe the different attributes of Allah. He believed that through meditating on any of these names, the true nature and essence of the godhead could be revealed. To him, all religious differences were merely the result of *maya* (illusion), and all forms of external religion were useless if the worshipper's heart remained immersed in the material world.

Guru Nanak was also an important social reformer. He stressed the pitiful plight of the *pariahs* (untouchables) and other low Hindu castes by emphasizing the *bhakti* (see pp.58–9) path to enlight-

THE LIFE OF GURU NANAK

Guru Nanak (1469–1539) was born at Talwandi near Lahore in the Punjab. His father was a minor government official and Nanak himself became an official in the service of the Sultan of Delhi. But despite his high status, and despite the fact that he witnessed the terrible brutality of the Mughal invasion, the cornerstones of his teaching were always equality before one god and reconciliation between Hindus and Muslims.

As a young man he worked for a while for the Mughal conquerors in Sultanpur, but after receiving a "revelation", he made pilgrimages to all the leading Hindu and Muslim shrines, including Mecca. He then returned to found a religious community in his native Punjab.

In the first decades of the 16th century, as Martin Luther was preaching reformation to the Christians of Europe, Guru Nanak preached unity and reform to a growing following in India. To them he was the source of all truth, and as a mark of their devotion they called themselves Sikhs, a name derived from the Sanskrit word for a disciple, *shishya*.

Guru Nanak was married and had two sons, but he chose Lehna, one of his closest followers, to be his successor. Lehna took the name Angad, after one of the lesser legendary

Guru Nanak, as portrayed in a 17th-century miniature painting.

heroes. All that he had learned from Guru Nanak is contained in the *Granth Sahib* (Book of the Lord), for which he devised a new script, *Gurmukhi*, to emphasize its sacred character.

enment, in which they, like everyone else, could achieve liberation through devotion to the godhead. In repudiation of what he saw as the iniquities of the caste system, he gave every Sikh the surname Singh ("Lion"), and established communal eating places in Sikh temples and communities, in which all his disciples were equal.

Nanak's teachings were collected into two books, the *Adi Granth* (the First Book) and the *Granth Sahib* (the Book of the Lord) by Angad, the second Sikh guru. Arjun, the fifth guru, was the first to die violently. After the death of the liberal emperor, Akbar, he gave money to Prince Khusru, the rebellious son of the new emperor, Jahangir. When

Arjun refused to pay the fine that was imposed on him in consequence, he was tortured to death. Thereafter, the Sikhs abandoned their pacificism and slowly evolved into a society of warriors. Under the tenth guru, Govind Singh, they were reconstituted as a military order.

The tenth guru was also the last. Before his assassination in 1708, Govind decreed that there should be no more gurus and that from then on the guruship and the earthly authority of the godhead should be vested in the *Granth Sahib*. The Sikhs have since divided into groups led by chiefs (Sirdars). Today, they are widely spread throughout India.

The Golden Temple at Amritsar in the Punjab is the premier shrine of Sikhism.

AMRITSAR

In 1579 the Mughal emperor Akbar granted a plot of land in the Punjab to the fourth Guru, Ram Das, so that the Sikhs could build themselves a capital. As a first step, Ram Das constructed a huge sacred water-tank, "the pool of nectar" (*Amrita Saras*), from which the city took its name. His successor, Arjun, built a temple on an island in the pool, and 200 years later the great Sikh ruler Ranjit Singh crowned it with a golden dome.

Punjab, in northwest India, is the Sanskrit word for "five rivers", a reference to the five tributaries of the Indus. Since the 16th century, Amritsar has been the Sikh capital.

Mahatma Gandhi

Mohandas Karamchand Gandhi (1869–1948) was the leading force behind the move for modern Indian independence. He claimed to be simply a seeker after truth, but in the eyes of Asia – and indeed most of the world – he was a great moral teacher, an uncompromising pacifist, a dauntless idealist and a passionate but humble patriot, truly worthy of the title Mahatma ("Great Soul").

The son of a rich hereditary minister in the government of Kathiawar in Gujarat, Gandhi studied law in London. But in 1893 he gave up a lucrative legal practice in Bombay and set out for South Africa, where he spent the next twenty-two years defending the rights of Indian immigrants, organizing public protests against the discrimina-tory injustices of the white government and acquiring a deep conviction that the only honourable road to political change lay in persuasion and direct but non-violent action.

In 1914 he returned to India, but before he threw himself wholeheartedly into the struggle for independence and the activities of the Indian National Congress party, he spent a year watch-ing and learning, and developing the teachings that were to direct the remainder of his life. The most impor-tant acknowledged influence on his teachings was the doctrine of *ahimsa* (non-violence), which originated in his native Gujurat. Gandhi found evidence of *ahimsa* in the Hindu *Bhagavad Gita* (see pp.60–61) and the Christian New Testament (particularly the Sermon on

In March 1930, Gandhi walked almost 250 miles (400km) from his home to the sea, to make salt in symbolic defiance of the British monopoly.

HOMESPUN CLOTH

In the 1920s Gandhi reintroduced the boycott and *swadeshi* movements, which had started in Bengal at the beginning of the century. The objectives were to damage the imperial economy by boycotting British goods, particularly cloth, and to develop economic independence by encouraging the manufacture of indigenous goods (*swadeshi*). Gandhi was also opposed to the use of labour-saving machines, which were "mere instruments of greed" and left many thousands of Indians out of work. Instead, he advocated the manufacture of homespun cloth.

Gandhi spinning khadi *cloth in a* harijan *colony in Delhi.*

the Mount), and in the writings of Saint Francis of Assisi, the Indian poet Raychandbhai, the English critic John Ruskin and the Russian novelist Leo Tolstoy, with whom he corresponded. From these sources Gandhi distilled a philosophy which centred on *satyagraha* (adherence to truth). "Truth", he wrote, "is the most important name of God." Just as he taught that there was no circumstance, however terrible, that could ever justify the use of violence, so he also taught that there was never any expediency that could justify the slightest deviation from truth. But these principles were neither negative nor passive. On the contrary, to Gandhi they were positive political weapons. If he could not persuade his opponents by reason or by disruptive non-cooperation, he would fast or willingly accept imprisonment, believing that through the example of his suffering he would eventually lead them to a change of heart and acceptance of his truth.

Gandhi was more concerned with changing human motives than with changing society. His dream of freedom for India did not end with independence. He also dreamed of freedom from materialism and freedom from the iniquities of the caste system. Before he began his new political campaign, he abandoned the Western clothes that he had worn in South Africa and took to wearing the loincloth (*dhoti*) that was worn by millions of Indian peasants.

In 1920, after a British general had ordered his Muslim and Buddhist soldiers to shoot down a peaceful Hindu crowd in Amritsar, Gandhi set out to make India ungovernable. For most of the next seventeen years, with the exception of several periods of imprisonment, he alternately defied and negotiated with the British and led the Indian people in a nation-wide campaign of civil disobedience. When victory finally came in 1947, however, it was tainted by the disappointment of partition. And within a year Gandhi had died at the hands of a Hindu assassin who had been angered by his efforts to bring about a reconciliation between Hindus and Muslims.

A statue of Mahatma Gandhi in Delhi.

Maharishi Mahesh Yogi

"I descended from the Himalayas with a technique that can lift the human mind and heart to heights where true knowledge ... can be fully realized. I call my technique meditation .... Through this, man can reach the innermost sphere of his existence in which life, essence, creativity, wisdom, peace and happiness reside." This is the promise that was given by Maharishi Mahesh Yogi, founder of Transcendental Meditation (TM).

Maharishi Mahesh Yogi is perhaps the most successful of all the gurus who have taken Hindu philosophy to the West. By 1994 there were over 1,200 TM centres in 108 countries around the world, employing more than 30,000 trained teachers. He has established two universities: the Maharishi European Research University in Switzerland and the Maharishi International University in Iowa, USA. His move-

Maharishi Mahesh Yogi in his later years, sitting before a picture of his master, the Shankaracharya (Swami Brahmananda).

ment has amassed such a fortune that when he bought Mentmore Towers, the huge country mansion in England that is now Europe's leading TM ashram, he was able to pay £25,000,000 for it.

The Maharishi was born Mahesh Varma in 1917. He studied with the guru Swami Brahmananda who, he claims, taught him the yogic technique that he later developed into TM. He founded the Spiritual Regeneration movement in 1957, and in 1959 set off for the United States where his success owed much to the secular, psychological nature of his doctrine, in contrast to the spiritual emphasis of other gurus.

He denied that TM is a religion and he made every effort to rid his movement of ritual and mysticism. Instead his aim was to "spontaneously unfold the full potential of the individual". His message of personal development and liberation could not have been more in keeping with the aspirations of 1960s America and Europe, although he condemned the use of hallucinogens. While many traditional Indian gurus demand renunciation of the world, the Maharishi showed a path of world-improvement through self-awareness. He promised only the liberation of human consciousness, not of the soul.

SWAMI MUKTANANDA

Swami Muktananda, the leader of a mission expounding the practice of Siddha Yoga, first met the Maharishi in Switzerland in 1975. He was an adept (*siddha*) of Kundalini Yoga (see pp.94–5) and his principal message was the yogic technique of meditation (*dhyana*). After his meeting with the Maharishi, followers of Muktananda claimed that not only had their teacher been granted the title of Adviser to the Dawn of the the Age of Enlightenment, but that the Maharishi had said that he enjoyed the highest state of consciousness. But soon after, relations between the two leaders appeared to have cooled and the Maharishi asked for all recordings of their conversations to be erased. In fact, Muktananda's teaching of Kundalini Yoga is far removed from the Maharishi's approach. His emphasis was on his personal ability to awaken the spiritual potential of his devotees all of whom had easy access to their master, in contrast to the Maharishi's attempts to focus his followers on his teaching as opposed to himself. But, as Muktananda observed, "Meditation is not a religion, nor is it the monopoly of any one country or creed. It is a

Guru Swami Muktananda.

way to peace. It is meant for everyone. God belongs to everyone equally. He is within you, he is you." Muktananda's most famous disciple is the American guru Da Love-Ananda.

THE BEATLES

Already famous, Maharishi Mahesh Yogi became a household name in the West when George Harrison of the Beatles became interested in his teachings. The Beatles and the actress Mia Farrow travelled to his ashram in the Himalayan foothills, accompanied by the eager cameras and pens of the world's press.

The Maharishi with some of his most famous disciples, including The Beatles, Mia Farrow and the singer Donovan, at his ashram in the Himalayas. Even though The Beatles' interest in TM later waned, the Maharishi's movement received a publicity boost from their visit.

Sai Baba

Sai Baba meeting some of his followers. His devotees, said to number fifty million worldwide, believe he is omnipresent and omniscient, and they call the present era the "Sai Age".

Sai Baba is by far the most famous of all the "holy men" in India. His devotees call him *Bhagwan* (God) and recognize him as an *avatar* (incarnation) of the Absolute (*brahman*) who has descended to earth in this corrupt era to restore *bhakti* (see pp.58–9) and righteousness. Sai Baba is an enigmatic figure, almost buried under the mass of largely mythological devotional literature that describes his life. He is best known for his miracles, the *siddhis*, which he claims as his "calling cards" and proof of his divinity.

Sai Baba's rise to fame was meteoric. In 1940, at the age of thirteen, he fell into a prolonged trance, punctuated by bouts of ecstatic laughter, crying and singing. Then one day he awoke and apparently began to materialize sweets and gifts for his neighbours and family, telling them that he was the incarnation

of the great Yogi Shirdi Sai Baba who had died a few years before. A series of magical exploits characterized his schooldays, and by the age of eighteen his growing band of devotees had begun to build his ashram in Andhra Pradesh. By 1990 he had about six million devotees in India, and fifty million across sixty-four countries worldwide.

Like his first incarnation, Sai Baba's followers are drawn from every caste, class, race and religion, and he claims that as an incarnation of the Absolute he transcends the limitations of each individual creed.

His cult is characterized by intense devotionalism (*bhakti*). Sai Baba's devotees do not revere him as a moral teacher or as a guru propounding a path to enlightenment, but believe him to be an embodiment of divine love. They are certain that he watches over them at all times, and that each of them is personally loved and cared for by this *avatar* of *brahman*. He is hardly ever seen in person yet his "powers" (*siddhis*) are said to enable him to appear at will in several places simultaneously, and to have a total vision that lets him see all things past, present and future.

Sai Baba's gift of divine love is symbolized by his most famous *siddhi* – the magical materialization of objects from thin air. He conjures up jewelry, sweets, perfumes, pictures of himself, and statues of various deities, seeming to pluck almost anything at random from the air. He then gives these items to his devotees as *prasad*, the sacred food or objects that a devotee leaves for a deity in a *puja* (see pp.104–5), to receive it again once it has been sanctified by contact with the divine. His *prasad* thus becomes a symbol of the love that the deity has for the devotee.

THE OTHER BABAS

The name Sai Baba (Divine Parent) represents the union of Shiva and Shakti, the twin principles of godhead. His present birth is the second of his three incarnations: the first – Yogi Shirdi Sai Baba – is said to be an *avatar* of Shakti; in his present incarnation he is Shiva and Shakti combined, and in his third life he will be born as Prem Sai, an incarnation of Shiva alone.

SACRED ASH

Sai Baba's most important *siddhi* is his materialization of sacred ash (*vibhuti*), of which he is said to produce more than one pound (0.5kg) a day, sometimes covering everything in a room. The ash symbolizes his previous incarnation – Yogi Shirdi Sai Baba – who offered devotees ash from his sacred fire. Many claims are made by Sai Baba's followers for the *vibhuti*'s healing powers. It is either eaten in small quantities or rubbed into an afflicted part of the body.

SHIRDI SAI BABA

Sai Baba's first incarnation was as the southern Indian guru Yogi Shirdi Sai Baba, who died in India in 1918. His birth is mysterious. He is said to have first appeared as a boy of sixteen who took his place at the foot of a sacred neem tree near a village in Maharashtra and stayed there meditating for three years. His fame as a yogi spread and it was not long before a band of devotees came to recognize his divinity. His followers were both Hindus and Muslims, and he embraced both religious traditions throughout the course of his life, teaching that everyone is equal and that "all gods are one". He was a Hatha Yogi

(see pp.88–9) who taught the Hindu way of yoga, sacrifice, penance and knowledge as the means to attain God, yet he spent much of his life in a mosque, being both a master of Hindu Vedanta philosophy and a worshipper of Allah, the God of Islam. As a Hatha Yogi, Shirdi Sai Baba kept a sacred fire (*dhuni*) burning at all times. He used to distribute the ash (*vibhuti*) from the fire to his devotees as a miraculous cure for disease and a magical elixir for inner transformation. Ash is also sacred to the Hindu deity Shiva, and is worn symbolically by his devotees.

A devotional statue of Shirdi Sai Baba in the southern Indian state of Maharashtra.

Rajneesh

Bhagwan (Lord) Shree Rajneesh arrived in the United States in 1981 proclaiming momentously: "I am the Messiah that America has been waiting for." Rajneesh spent only four years in the West, but during that time he became fabulously wealthy, establishing a 64,000-acre (260km^2) "city" for 5,000 devotees. But in 1985 he was ignominiously deported in handcuffs, and was sent back to his native India where he died in 1990.

Bhagwan Shree Rajneesh giving a typically charismatic sermon.

Born in 1931 in the state of Madhya Pradesh, the then Rajneesh Chandra Mohan was brought up by his grandparents as a Jain. He claims to have had his first taste of *samadhi* (ecstasy) when only seven years old and to have witnessed enlightenment as a psychic "explosion" at the age of twenty-one. He continued his studies and in 1958 became Professor of Philosophy at the University of Jabalpur, where he taught for nine years. During this time he toured India lecturing on Hindu and Western philosophy, constantly warning against the restrictions of mainstream religion. He finally resigned from the university in 1967 after a series of heated attacks on Hindu morality and social and sexual repression.

Rajneesh's adoption of the title Bhagwan in 1970 led to further controversy, as did the term *sannyasin* (monk) that he used for his highly unorthodox devotees. He became increasingly hostile to mainstream Hinduism, but his Western followers were by now arriving in their thousands at his Pune (Poonah) ashram in the state of Maharashtra. He stayed there for seven years, giving his followers daily discourses that have been published in 650 books and translated into thirty languages.

In 1981 he took a vow of silence before leaving secretly for the United States, where his followers bought a ranch in a small village in Oregon and set about building Rajneeshpuram, an ideal city. Its central hall held 25,000 people, and the complex included luxury hotels and a working farm. All were built by Rajneesh's devotees and the city thrived for a few years.

Rajneesh being driven in a Rolls-Royce through the streets of Rajneeshpuram in Oregon.

But by 1984, Rajneesh's mission was facing problems. He broke his vow of silence, but his talks now lacked their earlier brilliance. Rajneeshpuram more and more resembled an embattled camp, with guards patrolling its boundaries. Local people increasingly turned against his followers while his outspoken views on Christianity annoyed church leaders. Accused by the Federal authorities of arranging illicit marriages, Rajneesh was deported to India.

THE MYSTIC ROSE MEDITATION

One of Rajneesh's last creations was the Mystic Rose Meditation. This lasts for twenty-one days – a week of laughing for three hours a day, a week of crying for three hours a day and a week of witnessing for three hours a day. He claimed this as the "greatest breakthrough in meditation in 2,500 years". Rajneesh said that such techniques were essential to break down the ego and so liberate the enlightened mind. But some of his devotees claimed that they were used as guinea pigs in Rajneesh's increasingly random mental experiments.

RAJNEESH YOGA

Rajneesh's doctrine was an eclectic blend of Indian yoga and Western psychotherapy. Influenced by the mystics P.D. Ouspensky and G.I. Gurdjieff, he adapted the works of the psychologists C.G. Jung and R.D. Laing. He assumed the ordinary person to be fundamentally neurotic, divided and insecure, in need of spiritual guidance. Rajneesh taught that the way to be free of the ego is to confront directly emotional blocks and so transcend them. He used cathartic techniques, confronting his devotees with their neuroses. He preached a neo-Tantric philosophy about the power of sexual intercourse to release higher consciousness (see pp.110–11), and used to equate sexual love with

Rajneesh's followers wearing the obligatory orange dress of the sannyasin, *or renunciant, at an ecstatic prayer meeting.*

divine love. Rajneesh used sex as a way to break down guilt and inhibitions, arguing against celibacy as a tool with which to achieve spiritual enlightenment. "Morality is a false coin," he said. "It deceives people, it is not religion at all."

Krishna consciousness

Bhaktivedanta Swami Prabhupada published a total of ten million copies of the fifty books that he wrote during his lifetime. However, his name is far less well known than the name of the movement that he founded in 1969 – the International Society for Krishna Consciousness (ISKCON) – otherwise known as the "Hare Krishnas". The young devotees who distribute his books and pamphlets are a familiar sight in city streets throughout the world. Dancing, drumming and singing hymns in praise of Krishna (see pp.62–3), they are shaven-headed and dressed in saffron robes.

The theology of Krishna Consciousness is an offshoot from the ancient brand of ecstatic Vaishnavism (worship of Vishnu) taught by the great 15th-century yogi, Chaitanya. This saint was one of the leading exponents of *bhakti* (devotionalism), and its chief revivalist in eastern India. He was hailed as an *avatar* of Krishna in his own lifetime, and inaugurated the line of Vaishnavite gurus from which Swami Prabhupada

claims his origins. Chaitanya claimed to be the founder of the Baul sect, whose bands of religious singers and poets wandered India begging for food and following the yogic way of asceticism. Their ecstatic devotionalism was strongly influenced by Vaishnavite Tantra, which saw duality as illusory and taught that unity can be regained by symbolically uniting the twin principles of divinity in ritual sexual intercourse. The *bhakti* movement took this human love to be analogous with divine love, and worshipped Krishna with ecstatic trance, spirit possession and the devotional recitation of sacred chants and *mantras*.

Like so many of India's spiritual leaders, Swami Prabhupada's life is presented as a hagiography by his devotees. He was born in Calcutta in 1896 and named Abhaya Charan Dey. It is said that at his birth an astrologer predicted that he would leave India when he was seventy years old to propagate Krishna *bhakti* in the West. His parents were devout Vaishnavites, and he was

THE MAHAMANTRA

The "Hare Krishnas" derive their name from the Hindu *mahamantra*: Hare Krishna, Hare Krishna, Krishna Krishna, Hare Hare, Hare Rama, Hare Rama, Rama Rama, Hare Hare. This is the "great *mantra*" of Vaishnavism, incorporating the "power" (*shakti*) of both Krishna and Rama – the principal *avatars* of Vishnu.

ISKCON members in the UK in the grounds of their centre of worship, Bhaktivedanta Manor, at Letchmore Heath, Hertfordshire. The house was given to the society in 1973 by the pop singer George Harrison.

A festival chariot carrying images of Krishna, his brother and sister, attended by ISKCON followers.

brought up steeped in devotional literature, and as a strict vegetarian. He met Yogi Srila Bhaktisiddhanta Sarasvati in 1922, and ten years later was initiated as his disciple. Before his death in 1936, Prabhupada's guru instructed him to use his knowledge of English to write books and to "immerse the world in Krishna Consciousness". He left for the United States in 1965, and, on the crest of the Californian "flower power" movement, he established ISKCON in San Francisco.

Prabhupada taught a path of complete devotion to Krishna, and "the science of self-realization" whereby a life of abstinence and love opens the soul to Krishna Consciousness. Meat, eggs, alcohol, tea, coffee and other drugs are all banned, and sex is permitted only within marriage and for the sole purpose of procreation. Many Western followers claim not to be Hindus, and rather than recognizing Krishna as an *avatar* of Vishnu – and thus one of many Hindu deities – they hold him to be the "Supreme Personality of Godhead", the sole "God".

THE ACID GURU

Sri Bhakti Vijaya Acarya was one of the most senior Western leaders of ISKCON before he left to found his own "Order of Pilgrims" in 1977. He was Commissioner for the western United States, Kenya, South Africa, and much of western Europe. Many believe that the split from ISKCON was caused by Acarya's insistence that hallucinogenic drugs such as LSD can "awaken" Westerners immersed in the world of *maya* (illusion), and enhance their spiritual development. Acarya had spent several years with the American "acid guru" Timothy Leary, and was a key member of Leary's foundation and the San Francisco "League for Spiritual Discovery".

Pilgrimage Tours

The seven sacred cities

India's pilgrimage sites are known as *tirthas* (fords), crossings between the worldly and the divine spheres. A *tirtha* may be a river, such as the Ganges, or a mountain peak, such as Mount Kailasa – the mythical Himalayan retreat of Shiva. Shaivite *tirthas* may be naturally formed *lingas*, such as the Amarnath *linga* (see p.67). This is a stalagmite which attracts thousands of Hindu pilgrims every full-moon in August to a mountain cave near the border between India and Tibet. Several *tirthas* are places where the gods are believed to have descended to earth, and which may then act as gateways for the pilgrim to divine realms.

There are seven sacred cities in Hindu India, which are the principal pilgrimage centres: Varanasi and Hardwar on the river Ganges (see pp.162–3); Ayodhya, the birthplace of Rama; Mathura, Krishna's birthplace; Dwarka, where the adult Krishna ruled as king, and where Krishna Vasudeva was born (see p.62); Kanchipuram (see p.164), the great Shaivite temple city of Tamil Nadu; and Ujjain, site every twelve years of the Kumbha Mela festival (see p.162).

The most holy pilgrimage for a Hindu to make is around the four divine "abodes" that stand at the cardinal compass points of the mythological map of India: Badrinath, in the north, Puri in the east, Rameshwaram in the south and Dwarka in the west. Badrinath, high in the Himalayas, near the source of the river Ganges, has particular associations with Shiva, while both Puri and Dwarka are important to Krishna devotees. Puri holds the Rathayatra festival at the end of June, when thousands of worshippers draw through the streets massive temple chariots containing images of Jagannatha (a form of Krishna), his brother, Balarama, and sister, Subhadra. Rameshwaram is an island between mainland India and Sri Lanka, which Rama is said to have crossed on his journey to rescue his wife, Sita (see p.53).

Pilgrims descending Mount Shatrunjaya, the hill which "conquers enemies", one of the five holy mountains of Shvetambara Jainism.

The Ganges tour

The Ganges is India's most sacred river. Hindus believe its waters to have flowed eternally, for its source is said to be the summit of Mount Meru, the mythical mountain at the centre of the universe and the abode of the gods (see p.137). From there the river descends to earth via Shiva's matted hair, which cushions its fall. It is worshipped by Hindus as the goddess Ganga (see p.79) and the great cities of Varanasi, Allahabad and Hardwar on its banks are among the most important pilgrimage sites in India. Pilgrims bathe in the Ganges to cleanse themselves of the *karma* of previous and current lives, and so ensure an auspicious rebirth.

The closest temple to the source of the Ganges lies 10,300 feet (3,140m) up in the small mountain village of Gangotri, half a day's climb on foot from the pilgrimage town of Rishikesh. Gaumukh, the actual source of the Ganges is, at 13,858 feet (4,225m), a further day's walk away, to where the Gangotri glacier joins the Bhagirathi river. Prayer flags and small shrines mark the source, and ascetics inhabit some of the nearby caves, meditating in solitude. The nearby temple at Kedarnath, lying at 11,742 feet (3,580m), is a renowned pilgrimage site for Shiva devotees, as are the hot springs and temple at Badrinath, situated in a valley that runs between the Nar Parbat and Narayana Parbat peaks.

The Ganges' course across the plains to the Bay of Bengal begins at Hardwar, one of the seven sacred cities of Hindu India (see p.161). The river descends from the mountains through a narrow gorge, its main channel being marked by two stone lions. Hardwar's importance as a sacred site is derived from its position and the supposed spiritual purity of its water, which is carried by pilgrims to every corner of the subcontinent for use in purification ceremonies. Every twelve years the city is home to the great Kumbha Mela festival, when millions bathe in its sacred waters. This festival alternates between Hardwar, Ujjain, Nasik and Allahabad where, in 1989, over 15,000,000 pilgrims came to be cleansed. Allahabad is also known as Prayag ("Place of Sacrifice"), because Brahma is said to have performed a sacrifice there. Its importance as a great pilgrimage site derives from its situation at the confluence of the Ganges and Yamuna rivers and the mythical river Sarasvati, which is supposed to flow invisibly into the Ganges from its sacred underground course.

Varanasi attracts more pilgrims than any other sacred *tirtha* (ford) in India. Auspiciously situated on a bend of the Ganges where the river flows northward, its ancient name is Kashi ("City of Light"); it is presided over by Shiva in his manifestation as Vishvanatha, Lord of the Universe. The greatest of the many temples in the city is the Vishvanatha, and the Ganges water is said to symbolize Shiva's immanent power (*shakti*). Varanasi is also sacred to the Buddhists and the Jains. The historical Buddha visited the city and delivered his famous Deer Park sermon at nearby Sarnath (see p.34), while Mahavira, the founder of Jainism, lived in the city, as did the poet Kabir.

FAR LEFT *Built by the Nepalese general Amar Singh Thapa, the temple of Garhwal at Gangotri is the closest shrine to the Ganges' source; it is sacred to Ganga, Goddess of the River. The Hindu saint Raja Bhagirathi meditated here.*

LEFT *An old man ritually washes himself in the Ganges at Varanasi. Many Hindus come to Varanasi to bathe in the river before dying, believing that the holy water cleanses them of their sins.*

Central to Hindu beliefs and myths, the Ganges, rising in the Himalayas, flows through the very heart of India. Almost half of India's population live in its plain.

GANGES TOUR MAP

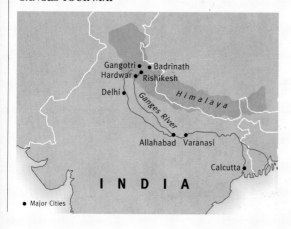

The southern Shiva tour

A good place to start a temple tour of southern India is at Mamallapuram (formerly Mahabalipuram) near Madras, on the eastern coast of Tamil Nadu. Mamallapuram is among the most picturesque of India's Hindu temple complexes. There are almost seventy rock-cut monoliths, caves and sculptures remaining, as well as the famous twin shore temples facing the sea on the village's beaches. Its rock-cut temples are the earliest examples of monumental architecture in southern India, and its rock art is certainly the finest that survives from the Pallava empire, which ruled much of south India between the 4th and 9th centuries AD.

A little further north is the great temple city of Kanchipuram, the capital of the Pallava and, from the 9th to 13th centuries AD, the Chola dynasties. Kanchipuram is honoured as one of the seven sacred cities in India, and has over 150 functioning temples dedicated to various Hindu deities. It is, however, predominantly a Shaivite centre. Among its best-known temples are the Kailashanatha complex, dedicated to Shiva Nataraja and Durga, and the Ekambareshvara Shiva temple.

It is said that the five elements (earth, water, fire, air and ether) are represented by five temple *lingas* in southern India. Visiting each has become an important act of pilgrimage for Shiva worshippers. The first is the earth *linga* at Ekambareshvara in Kanchipuram. The second, the water *linga*, is located in the Jambukeshvara temple on the river island of Srirangam, near the temple city of Tiruchirapalli.

From the remarkable 7th-century AD rock temples at Mamallapuram to the magnificent temple complexes of the 17th century AD, southern India houses many of Hinduism's finest examples of temple art. They are unique not only for their scale and beauty: unlike many monuments in the north, South India's great temples are still living religious institutions, and important centres of art and learning.

The water *linga* is permanently immersed in a small tank that is fed by a natural spring.

Fire, the third *linga*, is worshipped at Tiruvannamalai, one of the largest Shiva temples in southern India. Tiruvannamalai is especially renowned for the great fire festival that is celebrated at the end of November. On the tenth and final night an enormous bonfire is lit to symbolize Shiva's mythical appearance as a column of flame.

The air or wind *linga* is at Kalahasti, which lies on the banks of the sacred river Svarnamukhi in southern Andhra Pradesh. Kalahasti was an important religious capital of the Vijayanagara dynasty. It is dominated by the Kalahastishvara temple in which the wind *linga* is housed.

The fifth element, space or ether, is represented by the *linga* in Chidambaram (see p.134), the great Chola temple dedicated to Shiva Nataraja and his blissful dance, the Ananda Tandava. The crystal Chidambaram *linga* is the most important of the five because it stands for the ethereal fifth face of Shiva that encompasses and transcends the other four.

Perhaps the greatest Shaivite temple in southern India is the Brihadishvara temple in Thanjavur, which was built by the Chola dynasty between the 9th and 13th centuries AD. Its massive *linga*, 12 feet (3.6m) high, is placed beneath the tallest *gopura* (gateway) of any southern temple, and its murals and bronzes are among the finest examples of Shaivite art.

The most significant rock carving to survive from the Pallava dynasty period at Mamallapuram is the 7th-century AD relief called Arjuna's Penance, *which depicts a scene from the life of the warrior-mystic who is the hero of the* Bhagavad Gita. *It is also known as* The Descent of the Ganges.

Jain and Buddhist tirthas

Many of the most sacred Jain and Buddhist *tirthas* (fords) lie in the Ganges basin, where Mahavira, the Jain saint, and the Buddha lived, taught and died. The world's principal Buddhist *tirtha* is Bodh Gaya, the shrine that marks the place of the Buddha's enlightenment (see pp.32–3). Bodh Gaya is 7 miles (12km) south of Gaya in the state of Bihar. The name Bihar is itself derived from the Sanskrit *vihara*, meaning Buddhist monastery. Gaya is also an important pilgrimage centre: the Vishnupada temple there is said to have been built upon a footprint left in stone by the Hindu deity Vishnu, and the temple gardens contain a banyan tree under which the Buddha supposedly sat in meditation for six years. The Mahabodhi temple in Bodh Gaya houses Buddhism's most famous sacred object – a descendant of the *bodhi* tree beneath whose shelter the Buddha attained enlightenment. Under the tree is the *vajrasana*, the diamond throne that marks the actual place of his liberation.

Six miles (10km) north of Varanasi in Uttar Pradesh is Sarnath, the deer park in which the Buddha delivered his first sermon (see p.34). The Damekh Stupa which marks the supposed exact spot stands over 100 feet (30m) high. Kushinagara, in eastern Uttar Pradesh, is the place where the historical Buddha died and was cremated, while the town of Lumbini, just over the Nepalese border, is the site of his birth.

Varanasi is also a major Jain *tirtha* and centre of pilgrimage. The twenty-third Jain Fordmaker, Parshva, is said to have been born and spent his early life there. It is supposedly the place where four other Fordmakers set off on their way to liberation. Nearby Ayodhya is connected with a variety of Jain saints, and is said to be the ancient capital of Bharata, the first Jain monarch. Twenty miles (32km) to the southeast of Patna, the ancient capital of the region of Bihar, is Pava – the place where Mahavira, the twenty-fourth *Tirthankara,* died. The white marble Jalmandir temple in the middle of a lotus pond marks the place of his cremation. Mahavira was born at Vaishali, 25 miles (40km) to the north of Patna.

There are five mountains sacred to the Jain Shvetambara sect: Abu, Girnar, Shatrunjaya, Samneta and the legendary Mount Ashtapada, scene of the first Fordmaker Rishabha's liberation. Mount Girnar is in western Gujarat, a short walk from the ancient capital, Junagadh. Its sixteen temples form the largest Jain temple complex dedicated to Neminatha, the twenty-second Fordmaker. The village of Dilwara on the summit of Mount Abu contains temples constructed of marble in honour of Rishabha and Neminatha.

Digambara ("sky-clad") Jain pilgrims ascend the "Big Hill" at Shravana Belgola for the Mahamastakabhisheka festival, which has been held only seventy times since the 10th century AD.

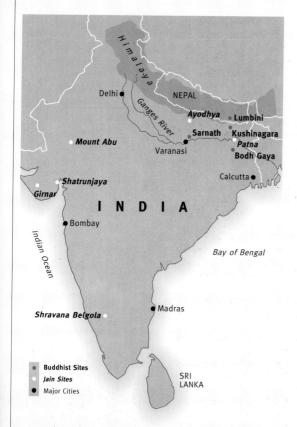

A map showing the distribution of the major Jain and Buddhist holy sites in India.

Mount Shatrunjaya, the hill which "conquers enemies", is two hours' climb from Palitana in Gujarat. The largest Shvetambara temple city in India, it has over 1,000 Jain shrines and 800 temples; visiting it is said to be as meritorious as visiting all other *tirthas* combined. It was supposedly built by Bharata, visited by Rishabha, and will be the site at which nineteen future Fordmakers will teach. Shravana Belgola, the Digambara sect's White Lake of the Ascetics, is midway between the cities of Mysore and Bangalore in Karnataka. Its Big Hill is dominated by the huge 57-foot (18m) image of Gommateshvara, said to be the first person to attain liberation. The adjacent Little Hill preceded the Gommateshvara image as a Digambara *tirtha*, and was a hallowed site for death by fasting (*sallekhana*).

Meditation

Understanding a yantra

Yantras derive their name from the Sanskrit, meaning "instrument", and are symbolic linear diagrams used by Tantrikas as aids to meditation (see p.110). They represent the various levels of creative energy (*shakti*) that radiate from the centre of the universe. This point of original creation is symbolized by a dot (*bindu*) at the *yantra*'s centre, while the various forms of energy are represented by different combinations of triangles, squares, pentagons and circles which go to make up a *yantra*.

The nine triangles of a Shri Yantra, for example, represent nine names of the goddess Devi (see pp.78–9); the five downward-pointing triangles denote the *yoni* (vulva), the four upward-pointing triangles the *linga* (phallus). Pentagons symbolize the five faces of Shiva, his five immanent *lingas* and the five elements (see pp.164–5). The triangle – and the colour triad of white, red and black – stands for the three functions of divinity: creation, preservation and dissolution, which are also the three "qualities" of material existence. This triad also embodies the Hindu trinity of Brahma, Vishnu and Shiva (see pp.48–9). The different basic colours used in a *yantra* indicate the purpose for which it was constructed – yellow and red generally signify a *yantra*'s positive power, while dark colours such as brown and blue are usually used for negative, destructive intent.

By meditating upon a *yantra*, these energies are internalized by the adept, so that they are transformed into levels of human consciousness. The meditator first concentrates upon a *yantra* and then closes his or her eyes and strives to visualize it in the mind's eye, finally imagining every detail of its outer form. At first, the novice visualizes complex *yantras* whose many rings represent the gross levels of consciousness (such as the emotions) to be transcended as meditation advances.

After visualizing complex *yantras*, the adept advances to more abstract diagrams. These emphasize the *bindu*, the

BASIC YANTRAS

The optical focus of a yantra *is the* bindu *(dot) at its centre. The* bindu *symbolizes the source of all creation, and the point to which everything returns.*

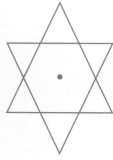

The bindu *here "resolves" the opposition of the upward and downward triangles.*

Each lotus petal of this 18th-century bronze amulet yantra *is inscribed with the Sanskrit name, or "seed", mantra of a Hindu deity.*

central point of the *yantra*. The *bindu* represents the centre of the cosmos, toward which all attention and consciousness are directed. Eventually, the meditator and the object of meditation become one, even the *bindu* dissolves and a union is forged between consciousness, the symbol and the cosmos.

Novices first master basic yogic techniques, such as elementary breath control (*pranayama*), to still the mind and develop concentration. A ritual, known as *pranapratistha*, is then used to infuse the *yantra* with "life force". This is achieved by consecrating the previously profane space that the *yantra* encloses with an exhalation through the right nostril, and by reciting a *mantra*.

Adepts begin meditating by fixing attention upon the *yantra*'s periphery, a square enclosure with four "doors" opening onto the four cardinal directions. The periphery represents passions such as anger, lust and fear. Through contemplation of these passions, the meditator overcomes them. Ascending through the gross levels of consciousness, represented by the outer rings of the *yantra*, the meditator transcends the physical self and begins the involution through the subtle inner rings and the gradual lightening of consciousness. Advanced adepts, however, do not use an exterior *yantra* but visualize the entire image, unfurling it from its central point, as the universe supposedly took shape from the *bindu* of creation. Once the diagram is fully visualized, the adept starts his or her meditation from the periphery and symbolically dissolves the material universe as he or she travels back to the central point.

Saluting the sun

Surya namaskar (saluting the sun) is an ancient practice designed to greet the primal energy (*shakti*) of the universe and invigorate the body at the beginning of a yoga session. It is practised just before dawn to harness the energy of the rising sun and stimulate the blood and abdominal organs.

Surya namaskar is a sequence of seven yogic *asanas* (postures) which the adept performs in quick succession as one "jump". The sequence should be repeated several times and should gradually get faster. The aim is to make it as smooth as possible, flowing from one position to the next, so that the jump seems to be made of a single downward motion, which is then reversed into a jump back upward to the starting point. The practitioner tries to synchronize each movement with his or her inhalations and exhalations.

1) The adept stands in the tadasana *position, with heels touching and hands pressed together in front of the chest in the* namaskar *(greeting posture).*

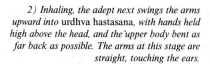

2) Inhaling, the adept next swings the arms upward into urdhva hastasana, *with hands held high above the head, and the upper body bent as far back as possible. The arms at this stage are straight, touching the ears.*

3) The adept then exhales and bends the body forward and downward into uttanasana. *The palms of the hands are placed on the ground beside the feet. The adept touches his or her knees with the nose, keeping the legs straight and the head looking at the floor.*

4) After inhaling, the adept takes the left leg backward as straight as possible so that the top of the foot lies on the floor. He or she then bends the right knee and draws it forward between the arms, placing the palms of the hands on the floor, in line with the right foot.

5) While exhaling, the adept "jumps" backward into adho mukha svanasana, pulling the right leg backward until both feet are placed alongside each other, with heels flat on the floor. The hips are raised and the chin should touch the chest. The head looks backward through the legs.

6) The adept next inhales and "jumps" downward into caturanga dandasana, taking the body's weight on his or her toes. The palms of the hands, the forehead, chest, knees and feet now come to rest on the floor, but the hips are slightly raised. The adept then exhales.

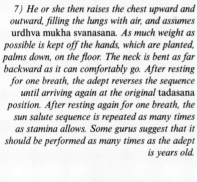

7) He or she then raises the chest upward and outward, filling the lungs with air, and assumes urdhva mukha svanasana. As much weight as possible is kept off the hands, which are planted, palms down, on the floor. The neck is bent as far backward as it can comfortably go. After resting for one breath, the adept reverses the sequence until arriving again at the original tadasana position. After resting again for one breath, the sun salute sequence is repeated as many times as stamina allows. Some gurus suggest that it should be performed as many times as the adept is years old.

Glossary

aghori class of *sadhus.*
Agni Vedic Lord of Fire.
ahimsa non-violence.
Alvar Tamil Vaishnavite saint.
Amman Mother Goddess of southern Indian villages.
anatman Buddhist concept of "not self".
Arhat Conqueror, a name of the Buddha.
arita non-order, chaos.
Arjun a hero of the *Bhagavad Gita;* ally of Krishna.
Aryans invaders of India in *c.*2500BC, authors of the *Vedas.*
asana "seat", position assumed for yoga.
ashram Hindu religious retreat.
Asuras demons, enemies of the Devas.
Atharvaveda the fourth *Veda,* composed for the fire priests.
atman "self", "spirit" or "soul".
avarna non-caste.
avatar incarnation of a deity, usually of Vishnu.
avidya Buddhist term meaning "ignorance".
Ayyappan southern Indian deity, born of Shiva and Vishnu.
banyan sacred tree.
betel stimulant used as offering to Hindu deities.
Bhagavad Gita "Song of the Lord", Book 6 of the *Mahabharata.*
Bhairava terrible and fearful aspect of Shiva.
bhakti Hindu devotionalism.
bhava artistic "mood", emotion.
bija "seed", as in "seed" *mantra.*
bindu central point from which all things emerged.
Boddhisattva "Buddha-to-be", a Buddhist saint.
bodhi tree of enlightenment under which the Buddha meditated.

Brahma Lord of Creation, one of the Hindu trinity.
brahmacharya chastity.
brahman the Absolute; Hindu concept of godhead.
Brahmanas ancient ritual texts, appendices to the *Vedas.*
Brahmasutras appendices to the *Upanishads.*
brahmin the priestly, and highest, of the four castes.
Buddha, the "Enlightened One", the historical figure Siddhartha Gautama.
Caitanya 16th-century Vaishnavite guru and saint.
chakra Vishnu's disc weapon; yogic energy centre.
Chinnamasta goddess of wisdom, aspect of Devi.
darshana sight, or viewing of temple deity.
Devas the gods.
Devi the Goddess.
dharma religious law, custom, duty or "truth".
dhunia *sadhu's* fire.
dhyana meditation.
Digambara Jain sect in which adepts go naked.
diksha Jain initiation into asceticism.
dukkha Buddhist term for suffering or imperfection.
Durga fierce goddess, aspect of Devi.
ganas Shiva's dwarf army.
Ganesha Remover of Obstacles, Shiva's elephant-headed son.
Ganga the river Ganges, also a goddess of the river Ganges.
garbhagriha sanctuary of a temple.
Garuda eagle mount of Vishnu.
gopis the cowherdesses beloved of Krishna.
gopura temple gateway with tower.
guru teacher, saint.
Hanuman monkey deity, ally of Rama.
Hatha Yoga the yoga of "force", the physical yoga.

Holi Hindu spring festival.
hrim "seed" *mantra* of Shiva.
ida energy channel, the left breath channel.
Indra Vedic king of the gods.
irrumudi cloth bag carried on heads of Ayyappan pilgrims.
Ishvara Hindu absolute deity.
jayikukka "becoming victorious"; Ayyappan's path to release.
jiva a Jain "conqueror" or saint.
jnana the way of knowledge.
jyotis naturally-forming Shiva *lingas.*
kala time.
Kali terrible Shaivite goddess of destruction.
Kali Yuga age of ignorance.
Kalki future world-saviour, incarnation of Vishnu.
kalpa a world age equivalent to a life of Brahma.
kama desire, deity of love.
karma action, the consequences resulting from past deeds.
kevala Jain "perfect wisdom".
krim Kali's "seed" *mantra.*
Krishna incarnation of Vishnu, popular hero of the *Mahabharata.*
kshatriya the warrior caste.
kundalini the serpent, a form of yoga.
laghiman levitation.
Lakshmi goddess, consort of Vishnu.
lila divine "play".
linga phallic emblem of Shiva.
loka the Hindu universe.
Mahabharata epic poem attributed to Vyasa.
mahasiddhi yogic powers.
Mahavira last of the twenty-four Jain Fordmakers.
Mahayana the predominant school of Buddhism.
Mahisura buffalo demon of ignorance.
Maitreya the future Buddha.
maladevas southern Indian forest demons.

mandala magical diagram representing consciousness and the cosmos.

mantra sacred syllable, ritual incantation.

maya illusion, mundane reality.

Meru mythical mountain, axis of the universe.

Mohini feminine form of Vishnu.

moksha release, liberation.

Muchilinda the serpent protector of the meditating Buddha.

mudra symbolic hand gesture.

Mukteshvara epithet of Shiva.

muni sage, ascetic.

Murugana southern Indian name for Skanda.

nadi energy channel.

Nagaraja king of the serpent deities.

nagas serpent deities and icons.

nagasveram southern Indian temple horn.

Nandi Shiva's bull mount.

Narasimha lion-headed incarnation of Vishnu.

Nataraja Lord of the Dance, an epithet of Shiva.

Nath Shaivite yogi, adept of Raja Yoga.

nirvana "extinguished"; Buddhist enlightenment.

Om sacred syllable from which the universe was created.

Pandavas the five brothers, heroes of the *Mahabharata.*

pariah "untouchable", non-caste Hindus.

Parshva the twenty-third Jain Fordmaker.

Parvati daughter of the Himalayas, consort of Shiva.

Patanjali author of the *Yoga Sutra.*

pingala energy channel, the right breath channel.

pradakshina clockwize ritual circumambulation.

pralaya destruction.

prana breath, subtle energy.

pranayama yogic discipline of breath or energy control.

prasad divine grace, ritual offering to deity.

puja worship of a deity.

Puranas sacred collection of legends and ritual practice.

purusha cosmic man, the spirit.

Radha Krishna's lover and favourite *gopi.*

ragas musical scales.

Raja Yoga "Royal Yoga" advocated by Patanjali.

Rama incarnation of Vishnu, popular hero of the *Ramayana.*

Ramayana epic story of Rama.

rasa artistic style, aesthetic "flavour".

Ravana demon king of Sri Lanka defeated by Rama.

Rigveda oldest and most venerated of the four *Vedas.*

rita order, structure.

rsis the "seers" who composed the *Vedas.*

Rudra Vedic deity, the Howler, possible prototype of Shiva.

sadhu ascetic, renunciant.

sahasrara the highest *chakra.*

samadhi internal ecstasy attained through meditation.

Samaveda the second *Veda,* a collection of ritual chants.

samsara the endless cycle of death and rebirth.

sangham Buddhist order or community of monks.

sanyasin a wandering ascetic, one engaged in the fourth stage of life.

Sarasvati goddess of wisdom, consort of Brahma.

sati ritual immolation of widows.

satyagraha "adherence to truth", mass non-violence.

Shaivite pertaining to Shiva.

shakti divine power incarnate in the Goddess.

shastra treatise prescribing correct conduct and practice.

Shiva principal Hindu deity, the Destroyer, Lord of Yoga.

shiva-shakti the male-female nature of godhead.

shudra the caste of labourers.

Shvetambara predominant Jain sect.

siddha yogic master.

siddhi yogic accomplishment.

Sita Rama's consort, heroine of the *Ramayana.*

Skanda the second son of Shiva and Parvati.

soma the mythical drink of the gods, elixir of immortality.

sunyata the Void, emptiness.

sushumna the central energy channel.

tabla Indian drum.

tala time, rhythm.

tantra a ritual path to release derived from the *Tantras.*

Tantras religious texts describing an esoteric path to enlightenment.

Tantrika practitioner of *tantra.*

tapas "inner heat" attained by ascetic discipline.

tirtha "ford" between mundane and divine realms.

Tirthankaras the Fordmakers, Jain saints.

trimurti the Hindu trilogy of Brahma, Vishnu and Shiva.

Upanishads philosophical appendices to the *Vedas.*

Vaishnavite pertaining to Vishnu.

Vaishyas devotees of Vishnu.

Valmiki reputed author of the *Ramayana.*

varnas the four castes.

Varuna Vedic warrior deity.

Vedas the most ancient and venerated Hindu texts.

Vedic pertaining to the *Vedas.*

vibhuti ash sacred to Shiva.

Vishnu the Preserver, one of the Hindu trinity.

Vritra Vedic demon.

Vyasa mythical sage and reputed composer of the *Mahabharata.*

Yajurveda the third *Veda.*

yaksha demi-god, tribal deity.

yantra symbolic diagram used as aid in meditation.

yoga a classical Indian philosophy and science of enlightenment.

yogi a practitioner of yoga.

yoni symbol of the vulva, emblem of Devi.

yuga a world age.

Bibliography

Bhardwaj, S. *Hindu Places of Pilgrimage in India* University of California Press, Berkeley, 1973

Bharati, A. *The Tantric Tradition* Rider, London, 1965

Brockington, J. *Hinduism – the Sacred Thread* Edinburgh University Press, Edinburgh, 1981

Clarke Warren, H. *Buddhism in Translation* Motilal Banarsidas, New Delhi, 1986

Clothey, F. *The Many Faces of Murukan* Mouton Publishers, The Hague, 1978

Conze, E. *Buddhist Meditation* Allen and Unwin, London and New York, 1956

Conze, E. (ed) *Buddhist Scriptures* Penguin, Harmondsworth and New York, 1959

Daniel, V. *Fluid Signs* University of California Press, Berkeley, 1984

Daniélou, A. *Hindu Polytheism* Princeton University Press, London and Princeton, 1964

Daniélou, A. *While the Gods Play* Inner Traditions International, Vermont, 1985

Das, H. *Tantrism: a Study of the Yogini Cult* Sterling, New Delhi, 1980

Dumont, L. *Religion, Politics and History of India* Mouton Publishers, Paris, 1970

Dundas, P. *The Jains* Routledge, London and New York, 1992

Eliade, M. *The Encyclopedia of Religion* Macmillan, New York, 1987

Eliade, M. *Images and Symbols – Studies in Religion* Harvill Press, London, 1961

Eliade, M. *Yoga, Immortality and Freedom* Princeton University Press, Princeton, 1969

Feuerstein, G. *Encyclopedic Dictionary of Yoga* Unwin Paperbacks, London, 1990

Feuerstein, G. *Holy Madness: Holy Fools and Rascal Gurus* Penguin, Harmondsworth, 1992, New York, 1991

Fouce, P. and Tomecko, D. *Shiva* Tamarind Press, Bangkok, 1990

Fuller, C. *The Camphor Flame* Princeton University Press, Princeton, 1992

Fuller, C. *Servants of the Goddess* Cambridge University Press, Cambridge, 1984

Gandhi, M. *The Story of My Experiment with Truth* Navajivan Publishers, Ahmedabad, 1940

Gordon, J. *The Golden Guru: the Strange Journey of Bhagwan Shree Rajneesh* Stephen Greene Press, Lexington, 1987

Hutchinson, R. *Yoga – a Way of Life* Hamlyn, London, 1974

Lemaitre, S. *Hinduism* Burns and Oates, London, 1959

Michell, G. *The Hindu Temple: an Introduction to its Meaning* Elek Books, London, 1977

Michell, G. *The Penguin Guide to the Monuments of India: Volume 1* Viking, London, 1989

Michell, G. (ed.) *Temple Towns of Tamil Nadu* Marg Publications, Bombay, 1993

Milne, H. *Bhagwan – the God that Failed* St Martin's Press, New York, 1986

Mookerjee, Ajit *Kali – the Feminine Force* Thames & Hudson, London, 1988

Mookerjee, Ajit *Kundalini* London 1982

Morris, B. *The Hill Pandaram* Athlone Press, London, 1982

O'Flaherty, Wendy *Asceticism and Eroticism in the Mythology of Siva* Oxford University Press, Oxford, 1973

O'Flaherty, Wendy *Hindu Myths – a sourcebook* Penguin, Harmondsworth and New York, 1975

O'Flaherty, Wendy *Karma and Rebirth in Classical Indian Traditions* University of California Press, Berkeley, 1980

Pandit, P.M. *Kundalini Yoga* Ganesh, Madras, 1979

Radhakrishnan, S. and Moore, C. *A Sourcebook in Indian Philosophy* Princeton University Press, Princeton, 1973

Rawson, P. *Tantra – the Indian cult of ecstasy* Thames & Hudson, London, 1973

Renou, L. *Religions of Ancient India* Athlone Press, London 1953, New York, 1954

Sahi, J. *The Child and the Serpent* Routledge, London and New York, 1980

Shearer, A. *Buddha – the Intelligent Heart* Thames & Hudson, London, 1992

Staal, F. *Exploring Mysticism* University of California Press, Berkeley, 1975

Stein, B. *The New Cambridge History of India* Cambridge University Press, Cambridge, 1990

Turner, E. and V. *Image and Pilgrimage in Christian Culture* Basil Blackwell, Oxford, 1978

Turner, V. *Dramas, Fields, and Metaphors* Cornell University Press, Ithaca, 1974

Vitebsky, P. *Dialogues with the Dead: the Discussion of Morality among the Sora of Eastern India* Cambridge University Press, Cambridge, 1993

Wasson, R. *Soma – Divine Mushroom of Immortality* Harcourt Brace Jovanovich, New York, 1968

Welbon, G. and Yocum, G. (eds) *Religious Festivals in South India & Sri Lanka* Manohar, New Delhi, 1982

Zaehner, R. *Hinduism* Oxford University Press, Oxford, 1962

Index

Page numbers indicate a
reference in the main text.
There may be references in
captions or feature boxes on
the same page. Page numbers in
italic indicate a reference in an
illustration caption only. Page
numbers in bold indicate a
reference in a feature box.

S

Picture credits

The publisher thanks the photographers and organizations for their kind permission to reproduce the following photographs in this book:

Abbreviations
B below; **C** centre; **T** top; **L** left; **R** right
DBP Duncan Baird Publishers

1 ffotograff /Jill Ranford; **2** Robert Harding Picture Library /David Beatty; **7** David Brittain from *Indian Style*;
Early India
8–9 Impact /Mike McQueen; **10T** Angelo Hornak; **10B** ET Archive; **11** Angelo Hornak; **12** Bridgeman Art Library/Oriental Museum, Durham University; **13L** Images/Charles Walker Collection; **13R** Barnaby's Picture Library; **14T** Mary Evans Picture Library; **14B** Ann & Bury Peerless; **15** Bridgeman Art Library / Victoria & Albert Museum, London;**16** By permission of the British Library (Or 4481); **17** Douglas Dickens; **18** Robert Harding Picture Library /K. Gillham; **19** Jean-Loup Charmet; **20L** Bridgeman Art Library /National Museum of India, New Delhi; **20R** ET Archive /National Museum, Karachi; **21TL** Robert Harding Picture Library /J. H. C. Wilson; **21TR** Michael Holford / Victoria and Albert Museum; **21B** Bruce Coleman /Gerald Cubitt; **22–3** By permission of the British Library (Add 5347); **24–5** Robert Harding Picture Library /Duncan Maxwell;
The Renunciation
26–7 Hutchison Library/Sue Dent; **28** Christophe Boisvieux; **29** Explorer /Manuel Garcia; **30T** Ann & Bury Peerless; **30B** Douglas Dickens; **31** The MacQuitty International Photographic Collection; **32** Robert Harding Picture Library / Adam Woolfitt; **33** Explorer /J. L. Nou; **34** ffotograff /Patricia Aithie; **35T** Michael Holford / Victoria & Albert Museum, London; **35B** Angelo Hornak /National Museum of India, New Delhi; **36T** Panos /Roderick Johnson; **36B** John Cleare Mountain Camera; **37** ffotograff /Patricia Aithie; **38** Mecky Fogeling; **39T** Bridgeman Art Library / Oriental Museum, Durham University; **39B** Angelo Hornak /National Museum of Indian, New Delhi; **40L** Christophe Boisvieux; **40R** Robert Harding Picture Library /J. H. C. Wilson; **41** Robert Harding Picture Library /Tony Gervis; **42T** Christophe Boisvieux; **42B** Images of India/Jeroen Snijders; **43T** Christophe Boisvieux; **43B** Angelo Hornak /National Museum of India, New Delhi; **44** Antonio Martinelli and R. Lazzeri; **45** Explorer /Christophe Boisvieux;

The Forms of Vishnu
46–7 Ann & Bury Peerless; **48L** Images /Charles Walker Collection; **48R** Angelo Hornak / National Museum of India, New Delhi; **49** Ann & Bury Peerless; **50** Jean-Loup Charmet; **51** Christophe Boisvieux; **52T** Robert Harding Picture Library /J. H. C. Wilson; **52B** Hutchison Library /Michael Macintyre; **53L** Bridgeman Art Library /National Museum of India, New Delhi; **53R** Ann & Bury Peerless; **54** Robert Harding Picture Library /J. H. C. Wilson; **55T** The Stapleton Collection; **55B** Hutchison Library / Patricio Goycoolea; **56** Mary Evans Picture Library; **57** By permission of the British Library (Add 16628); **58** Werner Forman Archive /Philip Goldman Collection, London; **59T** Copyright British Museum; **59C** ffotograff /Jill Ranford; **59B** Ann & Bury Peerless; **60** Impact /Mohamed Ansar; **61** By permission of the British Library (Or 13758); **62T** Spectrum Colour Library; **62BR** Explorer /Cajoom; **63BL** Angelo Hornak / National Museum of India, New Delhi; **63C** Ann & Bury Peerless; **63B** Ann & Bury Peerless;
Shiva and the Goddess
64–5 Copyright British Museum; **66T** Hutchison Library; **66B** Werner Forman Archive /De Young Museum, San Francisco; **67T** Copyright British Museum; **67B** Images of India/Metha; **68** Robert Harding Picture Library; **68–9** Spectrum Colour Library; **69T** Ann & Bury Peerless; **69B** Hutchison Library /Christine Pemberton; **70T** Rex /Angus McDonald; **70B** Christophe Boisvieux; **71T** Hutchison Library /Dave Brinicombe; **71B** Rex /Angus McDonald; **72TL** Sudhir Kasliwal; **72TR** The MacQuitty International Photographic Collection; **72B** Impact /Mohamed Ansar; **73L** Hutchison Library /Dave Brinicombe; **73R** Aspect Picture Library /Kim Naylor; **74T** Jain Picture Publishers; **74B** Explorer /J. L. Nou; **75L** Robert Harding Picture Library /Ross Greetham; **75R** Ebenezer Pictures /James Heard; **76** Copyright British Museum; **77T** Dick Scott Stewart; **77B** Copyright British Museum; **78** Copyright British Museum; **79T** Copyright British Museum; **79B** Impact / Mark Henley; **80T** Bridgeman Art Library; **80B** Bridgeman Art Library /National Museum of India, New Delhi; **81T** Explorer /J. L. Nou; **81BR** Angelo Hornak /National Museum of India, New Delhi; **81BL** Jain Picture Publishers;
Yogic Arts
82–3 Bridgeman Art Library /Private Collection; **84** Ann & Bury Peerless; **85** Jain Picture

Publishers; **86** Aspect Picture Library; **87** By permission of the British Library (Add 26433b); **88** By permission of the British Library (Or 24099); **89T** Images /Charles Walker Collection; **89B** Hutchison Library /Maurice Harvey; **90T** Robert Harding Picture Library /J. H. C. Wilson; **90B** Topham Picture Source; **91T** Douglas Dickens; **91B** Ann & Bury Peerless; **93** Images /Charles Walker Collection; **94** Jean-Loup Charmet; **95** Images /Charles Walker Collection; **96** ET Archive /Victoria & Albert Museum, London; **97L** Antonio Martinelli; **97R** Bridgeman Art Library /Private Collection; **98** Robert Harding Picture Library /N. A. Callow; **99** Robert Estall Photographs /Dale Heaton; **100** Ajit Mookerjee (now in the National Museum of India, New Delhi); **101** Agence Top /Edouard Boubat;

Ritual and Performance
102–3 Rex Features; **104** Robert Harding Picture Library /J. H. C. Wilson; **105T** Dick Waghorne; **105B** Hutchison Library /Patricio Goycoolea; **106** Robert Harding Picture Library /J. H. C. Wilson; **106–7** Rex Features; **107** Rex Features / Sipa; **108** Copyright British Museum; **108–9** Ann & Bury Peerless; **109** Hutchison Library / Christine Pemberton; **110** Images /Charles Walker Collection; **111L** Images /Charles Walker Collection; **111R** John Cleare Mountain Camera; **112** Copyright British Museum; **112–13** Agence Top /François le d'Ascorn; **113T** Christophe Boisvieux; **113B** Spectrum Colour Library; **114** Bridgeman Art Library /Victoria & Albert Museum, London; **114–15** Bridgeman Art Library /Private Collection; **116T** Robert Harding Picture Library/ J. H. C. Wilson; **116C** Explorer / Chawda/Photo Researchers; **116B** Christophe Boisvieux; **117T** Spectrum Colour Library; **117B** Zefa; **118T** Hutchison Library; **118B** Werner Forman Archive; **119L** Topham Picture Source; **119R** Impact /Ben Edwards; **120T** Explorer / Musée de Patra /J. L. Nou; **120B** Douglas Dickens; **121L** Images of India /Jeroen Snijders; **121R** Images of India /Jeroen Snijders;

Time and the Universe
122–3 Tony Stone Images/David Sutherland; **124–5** Hutchison Library /Patricio Goycoolea; **126L** Hutchison Library /Peter Montagnon; **126R** Hutchison Library /Patricio Goycoolea; **127L** Ann & Bury Peerless; **127R** Hutchison Library /John Hatt; **128** Ann & Bury Peerless; **129** Hutchison Library /Christine Pemberton; **130–31** Douglas Dickens; **132** Christophe Boisvieux; **133T** George Michell; **131B** Ann & Bury Peerless; **134T** Jules Selmes /DBP; **134B** Robert Harding Picture Library /Nigel

Cameron; **135** Copyright British Museum; **137** Antonio Martinelli and R. Lazzeri; **138** ET Archive /British Library; **139T** Images/Charles Walker Collection; **139B** Robert Estall; **140** Ann & Bury Peerless; **141L** Sudhir Kasliwal; **141R** Ann & Bury Peerless; **142–3** Images /Charles Walker Collection; **143** Michael Holford; **145** Robert Harding Picture Library/ Sybil Sassoon;

The Gurus
146–7 Hutchison Library /Juliet Highet; **148** Ann & Bury Peerless; **149** Spectrum Colour Library; **150** Popperfoto; **151T** Barnaby's Picture Library; **151B** Robert Harding Picture Library / Maurice Joseph; **152** Range /Bettman/UPI; **153T** Range / Bettman /UPI; **153B** The Hulton Deutsch Collection; **154** Christophe Boisvieux; **155** Dick Waghorne; **156T** Magnum /René Burri; **156B** Frank Spooner Pictures /Naythons /Liaison; **157** Rex Features /Brendon Beirne; **158–9** Hutchison Library /Liba Taylor;

Pilgrimage Tours
160 Christophe Boisvieux; **163L** John Cleare Mountain Camera; **163R** Robert Harding Picture Library /Adam Woolfitt; **165** Spectrum Colour Library; **166** Rex Features;

Meditation
169 Copyright British Museum.

Commissioned Illustrations

14R Line + Line; **20T** Sunita Singh; **43** Sunita Singh; **64BL** Line + Line; **73** Sunita Singh; **106B** Sunita Singh; **107B** Sunita Singh; **110** Sunita Singh; **120T** Sunita Singh; **121B** Sunita Singh; **149R** Line + Line; **163B** SLine + Line; **164** Line + Line; **167** Line + Line; **170** Ed Stuart; **171** Ed Stuart.

Every effort has been made to trace copyright holders. However, if there are any omissions we would be happy to insert them in future editions.